It CAN'T Be TRUE! 2

DK

LONDON, NEW YORK, MUNICH,
MELBOURNE, and DELHI

Senior editor Fleur Star
Senior art editor Rachael Grady
Editorial team Monica Byles, Katie John, Andrea Mills,
Vicky Richards, Caroline Stamps
US editor Margaret Parrish
Designers David Ball, Sheila Collins, Mik Gates,
Jemma Westing
Illustrators Chrissy Barnard, Adam Benton, Stuart
Jackson-Carter, Simon Mumford, Michael Parkin,
358 Jon @ KJA-Artists.com
Creative retouching Steve Crozier

Picture research Aditya Katyal

Jacket design Mark Cavanagh, Suhita Dharamjit,
Surabhi Wadhwa
Jacket editor Claire Gell
Senior DTP designer Harish Aggarwal
Managing jackets editor Saloni Singh
Jacket design development manager
Sophia M Tampakopoulos Turner

Producer (pre-production) Jacqueline Street
Production controller Vivienne Yong

Managing art editor Philip Letsu
Managing editor Francesca Baines
Publisher Andrew Macintyre
Art director Karen Self
Associate publishing director Liz Wheeler
Publishing director Jonathan Metcalf

First American Edition, 2016
Published in the United States by DK Publishing
345 Hudson Street, New York, New York 10014

Copyright © 2016 Dorling Kindersley Limited
DK, a Division of Penguin Random House LLC
16 17 18 19 20 10 9 8 7 6 5 4 3 2 1
001–288653–09/16

A catalog record for this book is available
from the Library of Congress.
ISBN: 978-1-4654-5407-2

DK books are available at special discounts when purchased
in bulk for sales promotions, premiums, fund-raising, or
educational use. For details, contact: DK Publishing Special
Markets, 345 Hudson Street, New York, New York 10014
SpecialSales@dk.com

Printed and bound in China

A WORLD OF IDEAS:
SEE ALL THERE IS TO KNOW

www.dk.com

CONTENTS

Planet Earth
and beyond

The natural world

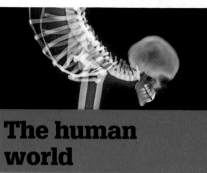

The human world

Feats of engineering

Planet Earth and beyond

Our planet is home to an array of picture-perfect panoramas, with sweeping forests, towering mountains, vast oceans, and skyscraping cities. It takes something truly out of this world to top them— the surrounding universe, with a star-studded spectacle of infinite wonders.

Weather and climate play a showstopping part in the evolution of Earth, influencing the lay of the land and affecting the lives of its people. Lightning strikes somewhere on Earth 100 times every second. Cities can experience major blackouts if a strike knocks out an electrical substation.

Boreal forests contain coniferous trees, such as pines and firs, and some deciduous trees, such as birch. ...

WOODED WORLD

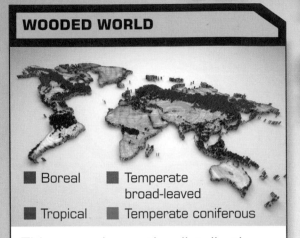

■ Boreal   ■ Temperate broad-leaved

■ Tropical   ■ Temperate coniferous

This map shows the distribution of forests in the world. Tropical forests grow near the equator, while boreal forests grow in cool, northern regions near the Arctic.

Temperate broad-leaved forests include trees such as oak, beech, and maple, which thrive in mild (or "temperate") climates.

Tropical rain forests have a year-round wet and warm climate, allowing trees such as the brazil nut to thrive and grow tall.

Temperate coniferous forests contain cone-bearing pine and fir trees, which are identified by their needle-shaped leaves. ...

If Earth's forests were put **together**, they would **cover** most of **North and South America.**

How many trees are there?

Forests cover nearly **one-third** of our planet's land. There are an estimated **3 trillion** trees on Earth, but **billions** of trees are being **lost every year** through deforestation.

Earth's forests currently measure around 15 million sq miles (40 million km²)—but every year an area the size of a small country is cleared to make room for people to grow crops or graze animals. Trees are also chopped down on an industrial scale to provide wood and paper.

Almost half of the forests in Australia are in Queensland, with much of the land protected as national parks.

Found mostly in Indonesia, Cambodia, Thailand, Myanmar, and Malaysia, the rain forests of Southeast Asia are the oldest tropical forests on Earth.

📈 FAST FACTS

Tropical forest makes up almost half of the world's trees. Boreal forest is nearly one-quarter, followed closely by temperate forest. Trees in other areas are the remaining 10 percent.

■ Tropical   ■ Boreal   ■ Temperate   ■ Other

For every person on Earth, there is a piece of forest the size of a soccer field and 400 trees.

What's the longest mountain range?

The **Mid-Ocean Ridge mountain chain** is **40,400 miles** (65,000 km) long, but almost all of it lies **deep** in the ocean.

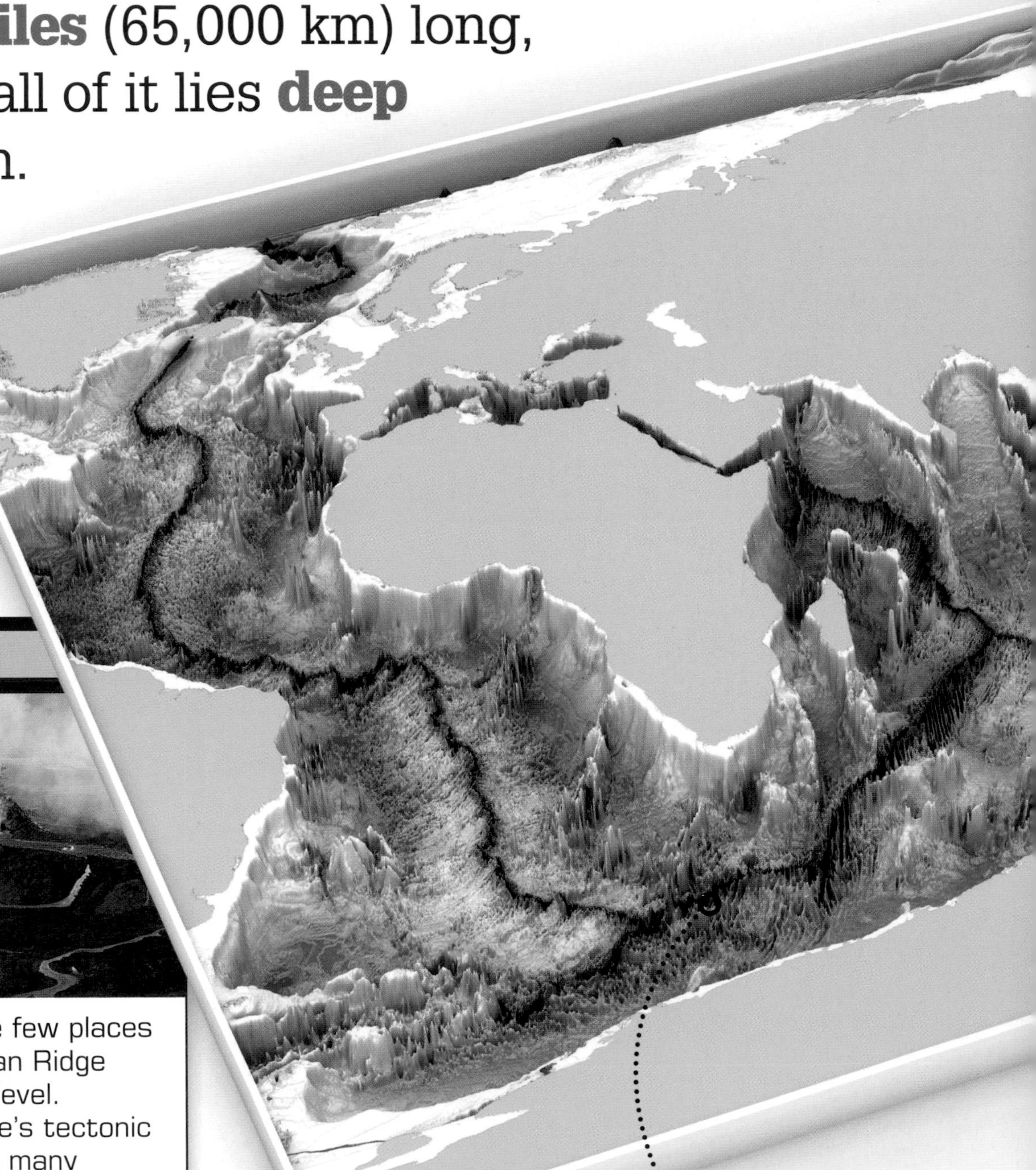

FIRE AND ICE

Iceland is one of the few places where the Mid-Ocean Ridge appears above sea level. Because of the ridge's tectonic activity, Iceland has many active volcanoes, such as Bardarbunga. This erupted for six months in 2014—2015.

Much of the Mid-Ocean Ridge remains unmapped, and existing charts may not be accurate because it is hard to map the seafloor.

The Mid-Ocean Ridge system formed along the joins between tectonic plates (sections of Earth's crust), which move continually. When the plates pull apart, magma from inside Earth's mantle comes to the surface and hardens into mountains.

The **Mid-Ocean Ridge system is** more than **nine times longer** than the **Andes.**

The Andes is the longest mountain range on land, stretching 4,350 miles (7,000 km) through seven countries in South America.

The top of the ridge is, on average, 8,200 ft (2,500 m) below sea level. Most volcanic eruptions around the ridge are so deep, they go unnoticed.

FAST FACTS

Earth is home to several large mountain ranges, with at least one on every major landmass. This chart shows the longest ranges on each continent.

Urals (Europe/Asia)
1,500 miles (2,400 km)

Transantarctic Mountains
(Antarctica) 2,175 miles (3,500 km)

Great Dividing Range
(Australia) 2,250 miles (3,600 km)

Himalayas/Karakoram/Hindu Kush
(Asia) 2,400 miles (3,800 km)

Great Escarpment
(Africa) 3,100 miles (5,000 km)

Rocky Mountains/Sierra Madre Oriental
(North America) 3,700 miles (6,000 km)

Andes
(South America) 4,350 miles (7,000 km)

How big is the Pacific Ocean?

The **Pacific** is Earth's **largest ocean**, covering about **one-third** of our planet's surface. Its area is about **62.5 million sq miles** (161,760,000 km^2).

North America

South America

Pacific Ocean

All the continents on Earth could fit inside the Pacific Basin.

The total area taken up by land on Earth is about 57 million sq miles (148 million km²).

Asia

Europe

Australasia

Africa

Antarctica

Water covers about two-thirds of Earth's surface, and half of this is in the Pacific Ocean.

PLASTIC PACIFIC

The Great Pacific Garbage Patch is an area up to 7 million sq miles (15 million km²) that contains trash—mostly plastic—that has been dumped in the ocean and swept together by the currents.

The Pacific Basin is slowly shrinking due to tectonic movement: some of the plates (pieces of Earth's crust) that make up the ocean floor are sliding under the continental plates that make up the land.

📈 FAST FACTS

The Ring of Fire is a zone around the edge of the Pacific that contains more than three-quarters of the world's volcanoes. Nine out of 10 earthquakes also take place here.

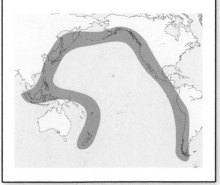

How much salt is in the sea?

If all the **salt** could be extracted from the **oceans** and put on **land**, it would cover the surface in a **layer** of salt **500 ft** (150 m) **thick**.

The world's oceans are salty because salt from the land enters the water as rivers pick up salt on the underlying rocks and soil and deposit it into the sea.

The total surface area of all the land on Earth is approximately 57.5 million sq miles (149 million km²).

📊 FAST FACTS

Salt makes up about 0.4 percent of a person's body weight. A 110-lb (50-kg) person has about ½ lb (200 g) of salt—that's 40 teaspoons.

A huge salt mine lies under the city of Detroit, Michigan. It is deep enough for New York's Chrysler Building to fit inside.

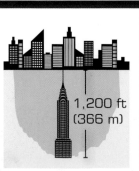

1,200 ft (366 m)

A cup of water from the Dead Sea—the world's saltiest water—has seven times more salt than a cup of water from the world's oceans.

PALACE OF SALT

The largest salt flat in the world is Salar de Uyuni in Bulivia, measuring 4,086 square miles (10,582 km²). This abundance of salt has led to a hotel constructed entirely from salt blocks. Palacio de Sal ("Palace of Salt") opened in 2007 with walls, floors, ceilings, and furniture all made from salt.

Salt from the oceans could create a crust on land taller than the Great Pyramid.

500 ft (150 m)

The salt crust would be the equivalent height of a 40-story office building.

The Great Pyramid of Giza in Egypt was completed in 2540 BCE.

Great Pyramid 482 ft (147 m) tall

How much rain falls in a year?

Planet Earth is a **wet world**, with a **total rainfall** of **121,000 cu miles** (505,000 km³). This includes other **precipitation**, such as sleet, snow, and hail.

FLOOD WARNING

When heavy rainfall makes a river burst its banks or causes water levels to rise, the resulting flood can destroy buildings and roads, and there is a risk to life.

Collected together, Earth's annual precipitation would form a ball 61.4 miles (98.8 km) high.

The average depth of rain across the whole planet for 1 year is almost 39 in (1 m)—about the height of a three-year-old child. However, less rain falls on land than over the oceans: on land, the average is 28 in (71.5cm).

FAST FACTS

Raindrops are not drop-shaped.

They are round when they start falling from the sky...

... But they change to a shape more like a hamburger bun as they collect and absorb other droplets on their way down to the ground.

Earth's **yearly rainfall** makes a sphere **11 times** the height of Everest.

Mount Everest's summit stands 29,029 ft (8,848 m) above sea level. It is the *highest* peak on Earth, but not the *tallest*: that is Mauna Kea, which is more than 33,000 ft (10,000 m) tall, but stands on the seabed so rises only 13,800 ft (4,205 m) above sea level.

How heavy is a cloud?

Scientists estimate that the **weight** of **water vapor** in a fluffy white **cumulus cloud** is **0.02 oz** (0.5 g) for every **35 cubic feet** (1 cubic meter) of cloud. This means that a ¼ **cubic mile** (1 km³) cloud weighs **550 tons** (500 metric tons).

A typical **cumulus cloud weighs** slightly more than **two Boeing 787 Dreamliners.**

TURBULENT TIMES

Air rises and falls inside clouds, creating swirling hot and cold currents. This can cause turbulence when airplanes fly through them, making the craft wobble and lose altitude.

The Boeing 78 Dreamliner ha a maximum takeo weight of 250 tor (228 metric tons

If a cloud is heavier than two aircraft, it is hard to imagine how it can float. The reason it does so is because the air underneath the cloud is denser than the cloud, and so holds it up. The weight of a cloud is spread out over billions of tiny water droplets. As these become heavier, the cloud breaks up and falls as rain.

A typical cumulus cloud contains 35 billion cu ft (1 billion m³) of water vapor, which weighs 1.1 million lb (half a billion grams).

Cumulus means "heap" in Latin and refers to the cloud's resemblance to a pile of cotton balls.

A cumulus cloud is a pocket of rising warm air containing water vapor. It expands and cools while gaining height in the sky. When the temperature cools to the dew point (when dew forms), it condenses into water droplets, forming a cloud.

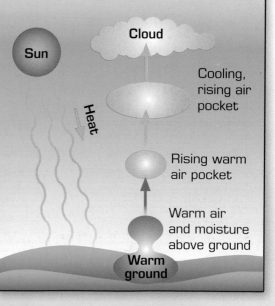

Sun

Cloud

Cooling, rising air pocket

Heat

Rising warm air pocket

Warm air and moisture above ground

Warm ground

How much electricity is in a lightning bolt?

Physicists estimate that more than **5 billion joules (J)** of energy are released in a **lightning bolt**—enough to meet the **monthly needs** of a **household**.

Making toast from lightning bolts is an impossible dream because the energy cannot be harnessed. No one can predict where lightning will strike, and the energy cannot be stored and converted into the safe "alternating current" used in houses.

THUNDERSTORMS

Much of the energy in lightning is released as heat. This warms up the surrounding air, which expands quickly and creates the sound of thunder.

One **lightning bolt** could, in theory, toast **100,000 slices** of **bread**.

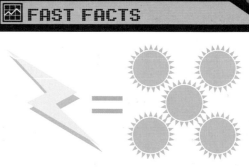

At 30,000 Kelvin (53,540 °F/ 29,730 °C), a lightning bolt is five times hotter than the surface of the Sun, which is 6,000 Kelvin (10,340 °F/5,730 °C).

The electricity in lightning moves at a superfast speed of 62 million mph (38.5 million kph).

In theory, 5 billion joules could power a 1,000-watt toaster for 1,400 hours, which is 1 minute, 40 seconds to toast two slices.

How long would it take to fall to the center of Earth?

Even though it is a physical impossibility, calculations suggest it would take about **19 minutes** to fall to Earth's core, traveling at up to **18,000 mph** (29,000 kph).

Why is it impossible? First, no one could dig a tunnel through Earth to its core. This calculation also assumes there is no air resistance in the tunnel: resistance would make the falling speed slower. Finally, if someone actually made it close to the center of Earth, the extremely hot temperatures would kill that person instantly.

Earth's crust consists of a variety of different types of rock on land and under the sea.

FAST FACTS

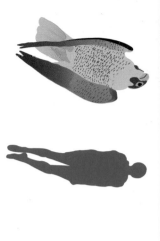

If a skydiver lies "flat" on the air, with arms and legs outstretched, he could reach a top speed of about 122 mph (195 kph)—as fast as a gyrfalcon when it dives.

If a skydiver pulls his limbs into the body to become more aerodynamic, speeds reach 200 mph (320 kph)—the same as a diving peregrine falcon.

It would take 19 minutes to fall 3,950 miles (6,357 km) to Earth's core.

The mantle is about 1,795 miles (2,890 km) thick and is mostly solid rock, parts of which can very slowly deform and move.

As the person approaches the center of Earth, the gravitational force would lessen because there is less mass beneath them and more mass above them.

In Earth's inner core, the temperature is about 10,800 °F (6,000 °C), the same as on the Sun's surface.

3,950 miles (6,357 km)

Earth data

MASSIVE VOLCANO

THE LARGEST SHIELD VOLCANO

on Earth is *under the Pacific Ocean*, **1,000 miles** (1,600 km) east of Japan. **Tamu Massif** covers **120,000 sq miles** (10,800 km²)—the same area as Thailand.

THE LARGEST ONLAND VOLCANO,

Mauna Loa, is one-sixtieth of Tamu Massif's size at **2,000 sq miles** (5,180 km³) in area.

Mauna Loa

EARTH'S *MAGNETIC* FIEL

▶ Earth's **magnetic field** is created by the molten iron in Earth's outer core moving around. As the molten iron moves, so does the magnetic field.

▶ Earth's **magnetic poles** move about 10 miles (16 km) a year. Since the early 19th century, magnetic north has moved northward by more than **600 miles** (1,000 km). In recent years the speed has increased to **24 miles** (40 km) per year.

▶ Every **few hundred thousand years**, the magnetic poles reverse. When this happens, if you held a compass with the needle *pointing to "N,"* it would actually be *pointing south*. These reversals take hundreds or thousands of years—the last one occurred about **780,000** years ago.

N

S

EARTH'S ROTATION

- The Earth takes **24 hours** to complete **one rotation** on its axis—in other words, one day. At the **equator** (24,900 miles/40,075 km long), the speed of the Earth's rotation is **1,040 mph** (1,675 kph)—roughly *twice the speed* of a cruising **airliner**.

- The time taken for each of Earth's rotations is **decreasing**, by about **1.4 milliseconds per 100 years**. At the moment, scientists adjust for this by adding **"leap seconds"** to standard time every few years.

Tajikistan is the highest country in the world, with an average elevation of **10,453 ft** (3,186 m) above sea level.

highest AND LOWEST

The world's **lowest country** is the Maldives, which is a tiny **6 ft** (1.8 m) above sea level—the height of an average man.

DRIEST PLACES

- The **driest** place on Earth is in **Antarctica**. The **McMurdo Dry Valleys** region has been almost completely swept free of ice by the extreme winds rushing over the landscape, melting any snow and ice.

- The **driest** non-polar area is the **Atacama Desert**, in Chile, which has an average of only 0.04 in (1 mm) of rain a year. Some parts of the desert have seen no rainfall for centuries.

BIOMASS

The biomass (the total mass of living things in a particular ecosystem) of adult humans on Earth has been estimated as **365 million tons** (332 million metric tons). We are *outweighed* by tiny Antarctic krill, which have an estimated total biomass of **420 million tons** (380 million metric tons).

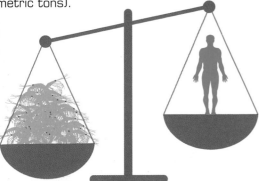

SPEEDY TSUNAMI

A **tsunami** (which is Japanese for *"harbor wave"*) can cross the **Pacific Ocean** in less than a day. It zips across the water at up to **600 mph** (970 kph), which is faster than a Boeing 777.

How far away is the Moon?

The average distance from Earth to the Moon is **237,675 miles** (382,500 km), but this can grow to **251,655 miles** (405,000 km) when they are at their **farthest apart**.

The rest of planets in the solar system could fit between **Earth** and the **Moon**.

Together with Earth, Mercury, Venus, and Mars are the four rocky planets.

From Earth....

Jupiter is a gas giant and the largest planet in the solar system. About 1,300 Earths could fit inside Jupiter.

FAST FACTS

The Moon's orbit around Earth is not circular, so its distance from Earth varies. If you drove to the Moon in a car at 70 mph (110 kph), it would take 133 days (4½ months) to arrive when the Moon is closest to Earth (at its perigee), or 149 days (5 months) when it is farthest away (at its apogee).

Perigee
233,700 miles
(360,000 km)

Apogee
251,655 miles
(405,000 km)

Added together, the diameters of Mercury, Venus, Mars, Jupiter, Saturn, Uranus, and Neptune total about 241,000 miles (388,000 km). They could easily fit between Earth and the Moon when they are at their farthest apart.

MOON FACE

Early astronomers mistook the dark areas of the Moon for water and called them "maria" (Latin for "seas"). They are ancient impact craters filled with solidified lava. The lighter areas are highland regions.

The Moon has about one-quarter of Earth's diameter.

Neptune is freezing cold, with some of the strongest winds in the solar system.

Uranus is blue because of methane gas in its atmosphere.

Saturn takes about 10 hours and 33 minutes to rotate on its axis. Earth takes 24 hours.

... to the Moon

How **high** can you **jump** in space?

The pull of **gravity** in **space** changes depending where you are. It's so weak on the **Moon**, you could **jump 5 ft 11 in** (181.4 cm) compared to just **12 in** (30 cm) on **Earth**.

The Moon has only one-eightieth of Earth's mass and its gravitational pu[ll] is 83 percent less.

Mercury has only about 38 percent of the gravity on Earth, so you can jump much higher.

Gravity on the Sun's surface is almost 30 times that on Earth. If you tried to jump, it would pull you back down.

Jumping on our planet results in a small lift before gravity pulls you back down to Earth.

SUN	**MERCURY**	**VENUS**	**EARTH**	**MOON**	**MARS**
0.42 inches (1.07 cm)	31 inches (79 cm)	13 inches (33.2 cm)	12 inches (30 cm)	71½ inches (181.4 cm)	31½ inches (79.8 cm)

FAST FACTS

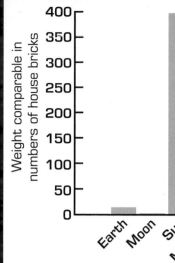

Weight comparable in numbers of house bricks: 400, 350, 300, 250, 200, 150, 100, 50, 0

Earth, Moon, Sun, Mercury, Venus, Mars, Jupiter, Saturn, Uranus, Neptune

Weight varies on other planets because of the gravitational pull: the stronger the pull, the more you weigh. This chart compares the weight of a 70-lb (32-kg) child in house bricks. On Earth he would weigh 14 bricks, but on the Sun he would weigh 28 times as much (if he could survive there).

If everyone on Earth jumped at the same time, the force would move our planet the slightest amount—$\frac{1}{100}$ of the width of a hydrogen atom—before moving back to where it was!

You can jump higher on the Moon than on any planet in the solar system.

FLOATING FREE

An orbiting spacecraft falls toward Earth, pulled by gravity. It also has a horizontal speed, so it ends up circling Earth. Because no force opposes the falling, astronauts on board the craft feel weightless and seem to float.

On supersized planet Jupiter, gravity is more than twice that of Earth, pulling you back down after only a small jump.

Saturn's gravity is only slightly more than that on Earth, so the jumping height is about the same.

Uranus is larger but less dense than Earth, with only 86 percent of our planet's surface gravity.

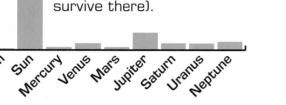

JUPITER
4¾ inches
(11.9 cm)

SATURN
11 inches
(28 cm)

URANUS
13½ inches
(33.7 cm)

NEPTUNE
10½ inches
(26.3 cm)

What is the hottest planet?

This chart shows the average temperatures at the solid surface of the rocky planets (Mercury, Venus, Earth, and Mars) and near the top of the atmosphere for the gas giants (Jupiter, Saturn, Uranus, and Neptune).

You might think that the **hottest planet** would be **Mercury**, as it is closest to the **Sun**, but the average surface temperature of **Venus** is **higher**, at **867.2 °F** (464 °C).

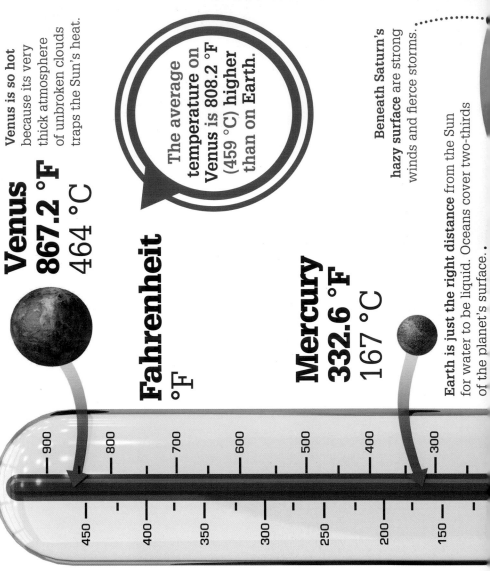

Venus
867.2 °F
464 °C

Venus is so hot because its very thick atmosphere of unbroken clouds traps the Sun's heat.

The average temperature on Venus is **808.2 °F** (459 °C) higher than on Earth.

Fahrenheit °F

Mercury
332.6 °F
167 °C

Earth is just the right distance from the Sun for water to be liquid. Oceans cover two-thirds of the planet's surface.

Beneath Saturn's hazy surface are strong winds and fierce storms.

900 — 450
800 — 400
700 — 350
600 — 300
500 — 250
400 — 200
300 — 150

Centigrade °C

Jupiter
- 166 °F
- 110 °C

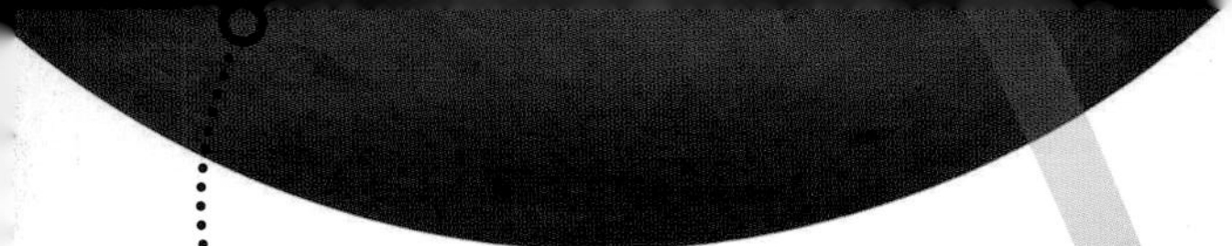

Cloudy spots on Jupiter are storms, which can rage for years.

Mars
-85 °F
-65 °C
Earth
59 °F
15 °C
Saturn
-220 °F
-140 °C
Uranus
-319 °F
-195 °C
Neptune
-328 °F
-200 °C
0
50
100
150
200
0
100
200
300

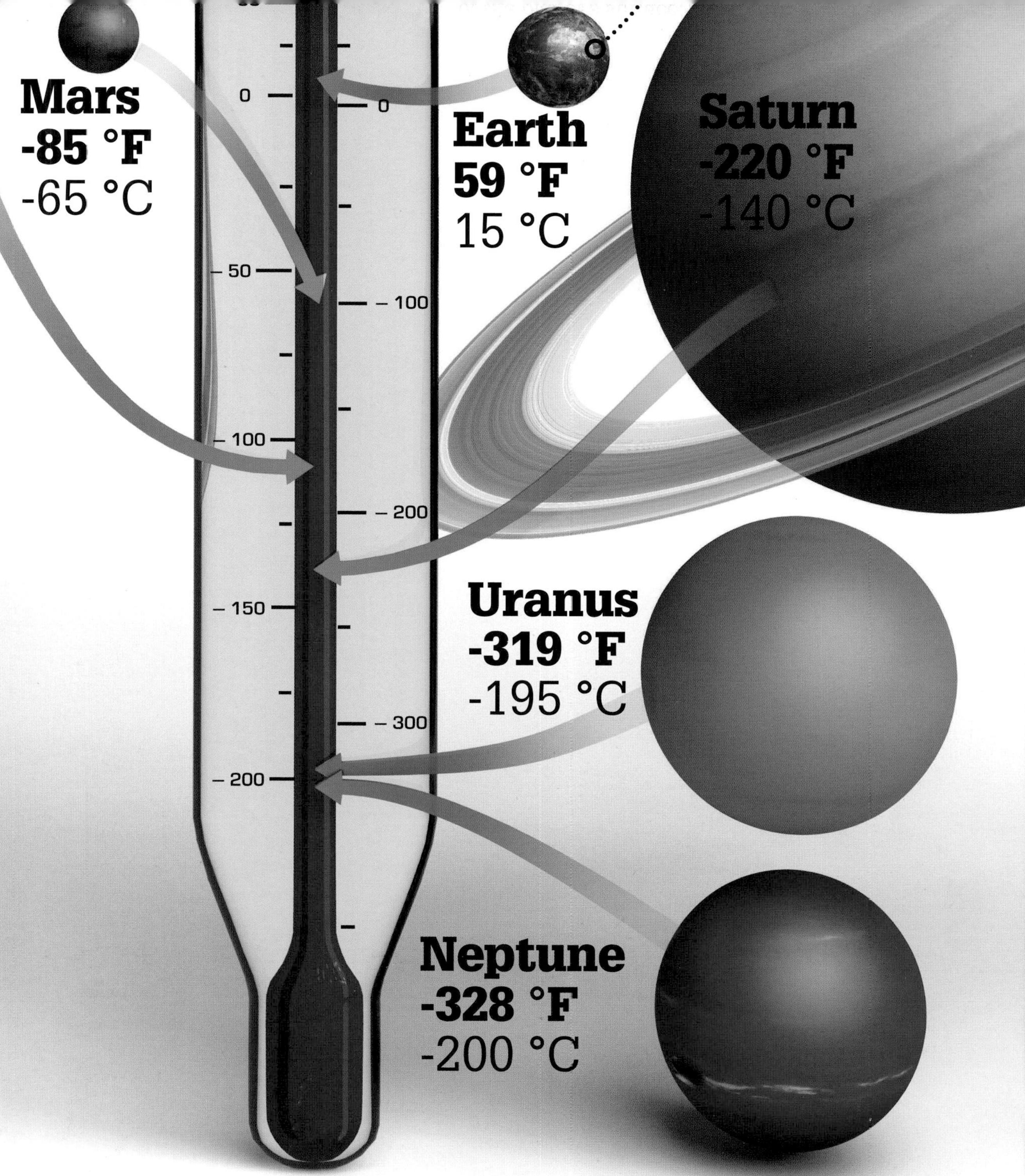

FAST FACTS

The hottest planet yet discovered outside our solar system, called Kepler-70b, is estimated to have a mind-melting surface temperature of a 13,398 °F (6,870 °C)—much hotter than the surface of the Sun.

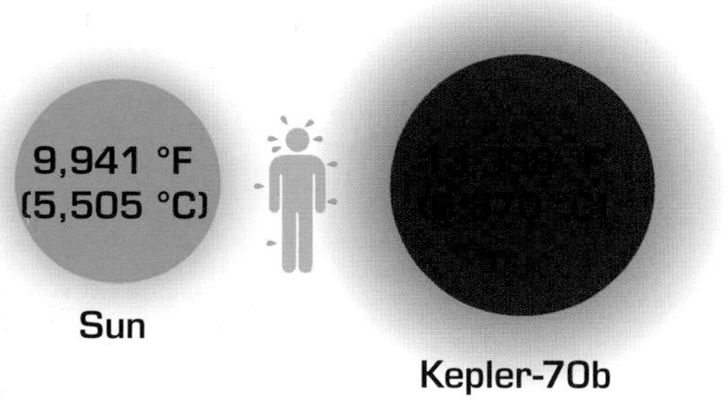

9,941 °F
(5,505 °C)
Sun
Kepler-70b

The pressure of Venus's atmosphere at its surface is 92 times the pressure at Earth's surface. It is the same as Earth's water pressure at 3,000 ft (900 m) under the sea.

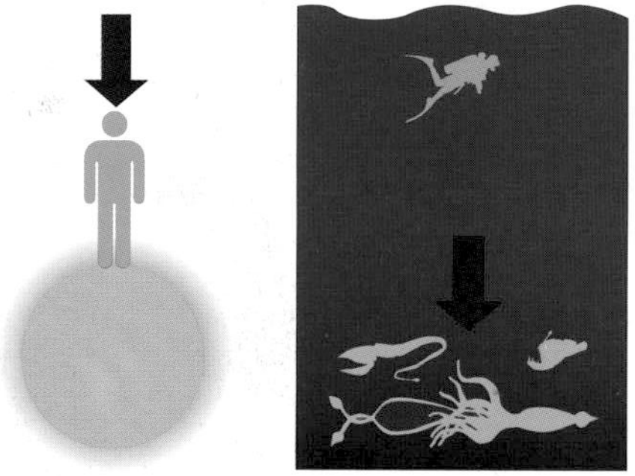

What's the most massive planet?

At **4,184,000,000,000,000,000,000,000,000 lb** (1,898,000,000,000,000,000,000,000,000 kg), **Jupiter** has the biggest planetary mass. If **Earth's mass** is represented by **one orange**, **Jupiter** is represented by **eight crates** of oranges.

MERCURY
0.05 × Earth

MARS
0.1 × Earth

VENUS
0.8 × Earth

URANUS
15 × Earth

EARTH
1 orange

........Earth's mass is near halfway in the planetary scale.

Although mass and weight are not the same, the masses of the solar system planets could be compared through some weighing experiments, as long as they were all weighed at the same location.

FAST FACTS

The Sun is by far the most massive object in the solar system, making up 99.86 percent of the entire solar system's mass, including all the planets, asteroids, and moons. Its mass is 4,385,000,000,000,000,000,000,000,000,000 lb (1,989,000,000,000,000,000,000,000,000,000 kg) or 333,000 Earths.

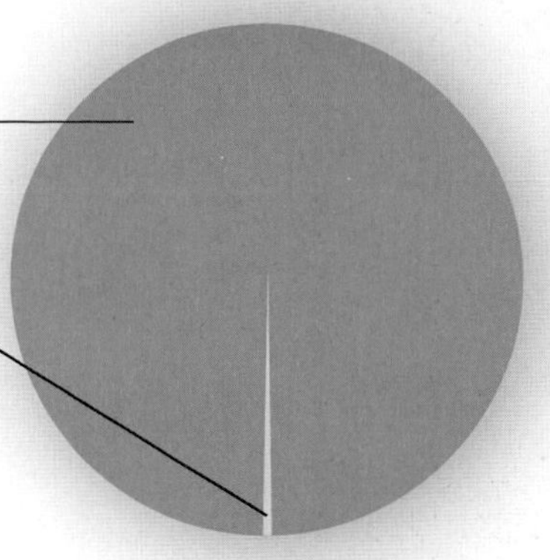

Sun's mass

Mass of everything else in the solar system

Each crate here contains approximately 40 oranges.

JUPITER
318 × Earth

SATURN
95 × Earth

The most massive planet is Jupiter, which has 318 times the mass of Earth.

NEPTUNE
17 × Earth

How big is Pluto?

Pluto is one of the **largest dwarf planets**, measuring **6,427,805 sq miles** (16,647,940 km²)— just **3.3 percent** of **Earth's area**.

Pluto is currently more than 3 billion miles (5 billion km) from Earth. A NASA spacecraft flew past Pluto in 2015, having set off from Earth in 2006. Light takes eight minutes to reach the Earth from the Sun, but at least four hours to travel from Pluto to Earth.

Pluto was downgraded from a planet to a dwarf planet—a round object in the solar system that is bigger than a comet or asteroid, but not planet-sized, and orbits the Sun.

FAST FACTS

Pluto is one of five recognized dwarf planets in our solar system, but experts estimate there may be about 50 altogether. The others are Eris (the biggest dwarf planet so far), Ceres, Haumea, and Makemake.

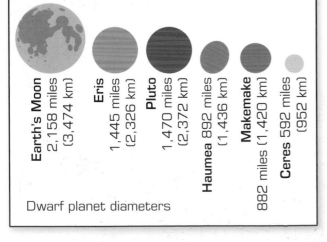

Earth's Moon 2,158 miles (3,474 km)

Eris 1,445 miles (2,326 km)

Pluto 1,470 miles (2,372 km)

Haumea 892 miles (1,436 km)

Makemake 882 miles (1,420 km)

Ceres 592 miles (952 km)

Dwarf planet diameters

ICY WORLD

Pluto's icy surface is made of frozen gases. This dwarf planet is very cold, with average surface temperatures of -393 °F (-236 °C). A mix of rock and ice makes up the interior.

Pluto is small enough to fit between San Francisco, California, and Austin, Texas

How large are Saturn's rings?

Saturn is the solar system's **second largest** planet, just over **nine times** the diameter of Earth. It is instantly recognizable by its **huge rings**, which are more than **174,000 miles** (280,000 km) wide.

There are seven main rings, with each one made up of hundreds of smaller ringlets.

The Cassini gap, named after its discoverer, is 2,900 miles (4,700 km) wide: big enough for Canada to fit inside.

Saturn's rings are made up of billions of pieces of ice and rock, ranging in size from tiny dust particles to huge lumps bigger than a house. Jupiter, Neptune, and Uranus also have rings, but they are much smaller.

FAST FACTS

There is room to fit 764 Earths inside Saturn.

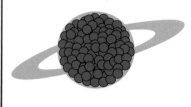

If you drove a car nonstop across Saturn's rings at 30 mph (50 kph), the journey would take 58 days.

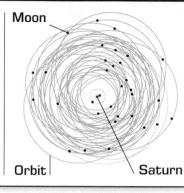

Moon

Orbit

Saturn

Saturn has 62 known moons. Many small, outer moons travel along tilted orbits far outside the planet's rings.

Beneath the haze around Saturn are strong winds and raging storms.

More than **21 Earths could fit across the diameter** of **Saturn's rings**.

RINGED WONDER

In 2009, a supersized ring of dust grains was discovered beyond Saturn's main rings. It covers an area almost 7,000 times larger than Saturn.

How big is Comet P67/C-G?

Comet P67/Churyumov Gerasimenko is **2.7 miles** (4.6 km) **long** and **2.5 miles** (4.1 km) **tall** at its biggest.

COMET COLOR

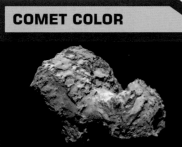

In space, the comet looks pale because it reflects sunlight in the darkness. If the comet were on Earth, it would appear dark against our lighter sky.

The comet's **highest** point is more than **12 times** the **height** of the **Eiffel Tower** in Paris.

FAST FACTS

In 2014, scientists landed a probe on the comet. It came from the spacecraft Rosetta, which was launched in 2004.

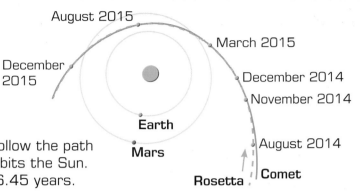

Rosetta will continue to follow the path of Comet P67/C-G as it orbits the Sun. One complete orbit takes 6.45 years.

The comet has two lobes (or parts), which suggests that two smaller bodies probably joined together.

Comet P67/Churyumov Gerasimenko was named after its Russian discoverers in 1969. Recently, spacecraft and probes have spent long periods studying its dusty surface and dark interior.

The coal-colored crust has an outer layer of carbon-based material. Inside, the comet's small core is a "dirty snowball" made up of ice and dust.

How much space junk is there?

More than **150 million** pieces of space junk are currently orbiting Earth. They have an estimated total mass of nearly **7,000 tons** (6,300 metric tons). Let's talk trash!

A small fleck of debris orbiting near Earth would have the same impact as a 550 lb (250 kg) object traveling at 60 mph (100 kph).

SPINNING SATELLITES

More than 6,600 satellites have been launched into orbit in the history of space exploration. About half are still there, but only about 1,000 of them are currently operating.

There are more than **650,000 pieces** of **debris** bigger than a **marble** orbiting Earth.

FAST FACTS

National space agencies have counted up the number of large objects they have in space. In 2012, Russia had the most.

6,000 objects
Russia

4,627 objects
USA

3,672 objects
China

The satellites and junk in space are influenced by gravity, which pulls them into traveling in orbits (paths) around Earth.

Earth

High Earth orbit 22,236 miles (35,786 km) from Earth

Mid Earth orbit 1,240– 22,236 miles (2,000–35,786 km) from Earth

Low Earth orbit up to 1,240 miles (2,000 km) from Earth

Satellites can be as close as 185 miles (300 km) from Earth, or as far away as 22,500 miles (36,000 km)—in a few cases, even farther.

Some 95 percent of space junk is debris that humans have left in space, including old satellites, used rocket parts, and fragments from erosion and collisions. The speed at which they travel means even a speck of dust or a fleck of paint can cause damage.

Space junk travels around Earth at speeds of up to 17,500 mph (28,100 kph).

Space exploration data

STARGAZING

On a **clear night**, with an unaided eye, it's possible to see around **2,500** STARS.

SPACE LIVING

The **International Space Station** orbits the Earth at about **17,500 mph** (28,000 kph). This means astronauts aboard the ISS see the **Sun rise and set** every 90 minutes.

ASTRONAUT STATUS

The **World Air Sports Federation** (FAI) recognizes only those flights that reach an altitude of **more than 60 miles** (100 km) as space flights. However, NASA awards astronaut wings to any astronauts who **travel above 50 miles** (80 km).

FIRST VOYAGES

The world's first artificial satellite—**Sputnik**, a Russian communications satellite—is launched. Later that year **Sputnik 2** launches, carrying a dog called Laika: the first animal to orbit Earth.

1957

Yuri Gagarin becomes the first human in space and orbits the Earth once during a **108-minute** flight.

1961

Neil Armstrong becomes the first person to set foot on the Moon.

1969

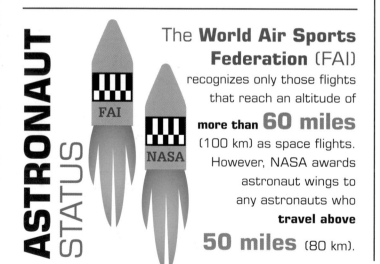

INESTIMABLY **HUGE** UNIVERSE

There are **more stars** in our universe than **grains of sand** on all of Earth's beaches.

ROCKET FUEL

The Space Shuttle was a spacecraft used to take astronauts into and back from space.

The Space Shuttle carried nearly **528,000 gallons** (2 million liters) of fuel just in its **external tank**. That's around **10,000 bathtubs of fuel**.

Each of the two **Solid Rocket Boosters** carried more than **1 million lb** (454,000 kg) **of solid propellant.**

SPACESUITS

• A space suit weighs **280 lb** (127 kg)—*without anyone in it!*

• It takes **45 minutes** to put on, including the *special clothes* worn underneath to keep the astronaut cool.

• An **oxygen supply** is *fanned* through the suit so the *astronaut can breathe.*

• The suit is **pressurized**—it squeezes the astronaut's body to stop his or her body fluids from *boiling in space*.

• The helmet's **visor** has a layer of *gold* to *protect against the Sun's rays.*

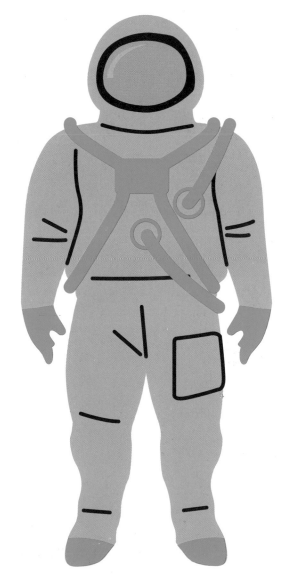

The natural world

From the birds soaring above our heads to the insects scuttling beneath our feet, the animal kingdom has much more to offer than the few creatures we know about. The number of animal species is in excess of 7 million, including some astonishing animals with curious qualities.

Owls are formidable hunters, with heightened senses and killer instincts. The great gray owl has superb long-distance vision coupled with specialized ears to detect moving prey. This big bird can even locate a target beneath 2 ft (0.6 m) of snow.

What's the smallest frog?

The world's smallest frog, ***Paedophryne amauensis***, is just over ¼ in (7.7 mm) long—about the **size of a fly**. It is not only the smallest frog, but also the **smallest vertebrate** (animal with a backbone). It was discovered in Papua New Guinea in 2009.

The *Paedophryne amauensis* frog is small enough to sit on a dime.

Life-size frog and dime

📊 FAST FACTS

The biggest species of frog is the Goliath, which comes from Africa. It is more than two-thirds the length of a house cat. It would take 41½ *Paedophryne amauensis* frogs to make a line of the same length.

Average house cat
18 in (46 cm)

Goliath frog
12½ in (32 cm)

A dime is just under ¾ in (17.9 mm) wide. It is worth 10 cents, but costs more than five cents to make.

With back legs that are longer than its body when outstretched, the frog can jump 30 times its body length.

The see-through skin of a glass frog's abdomen reveals its inner organs. Seen from above, the rest of its skin is lime-green— ideal camouflage among leaves.

Most frogs start life in water as tadpoles, but this species lives only on land. Its young do not have a tadpole stage but are born as "hoppers"— even tinier versions of the adult frog.

What's the biggest dog?

The tallest dog in the world was **Zeus**, a **Great Dane** towering **3¾ ft** (1.12 m) from the ground to his shoulders. A gentle giant, Zeus worked as a **therapy dog**, visiting schools and hospitals.

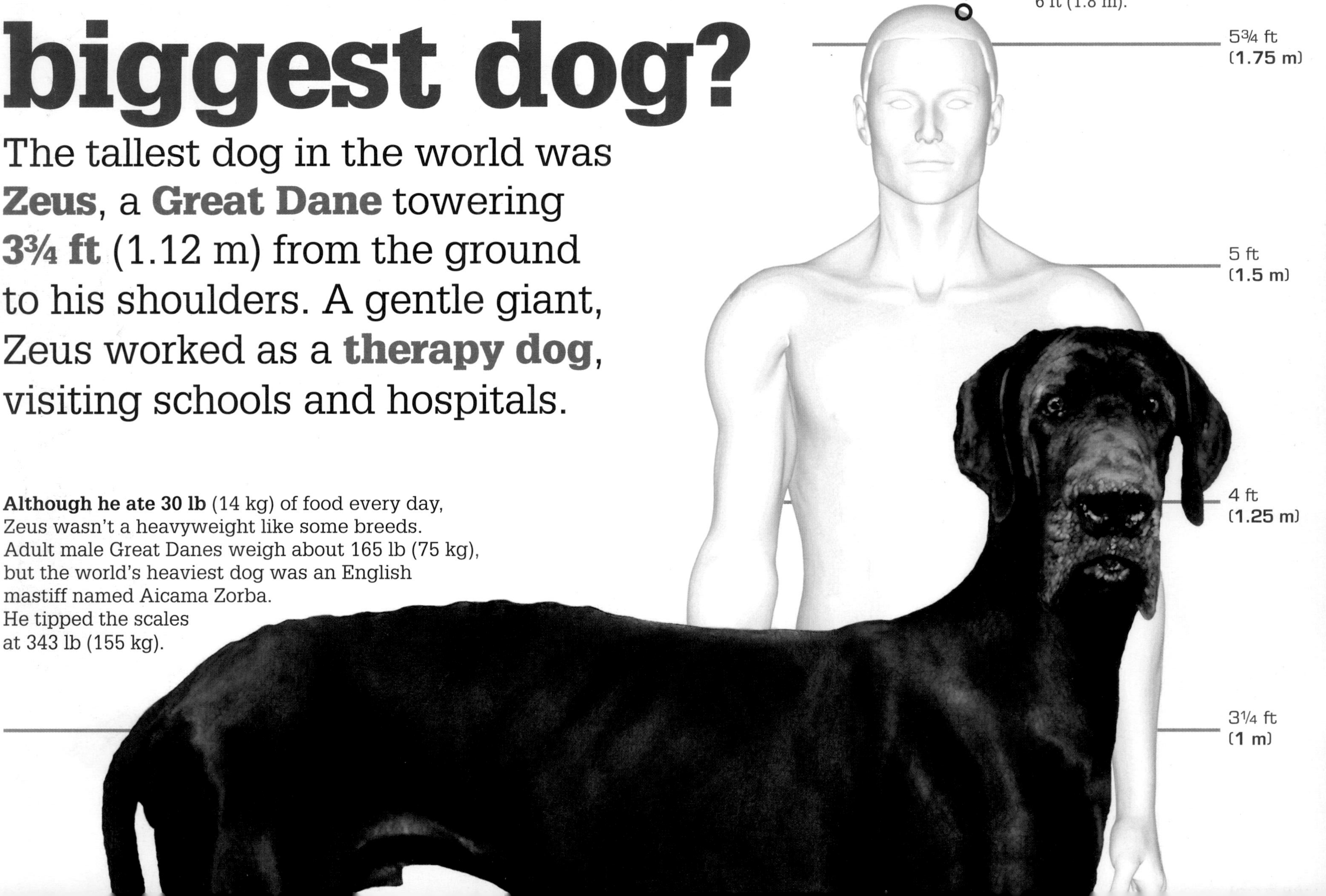

Although he ate 30 lb (14 kg) of food every day, Zeus wasn't a heavyweight like some breeds. Adult male Great Danes weigh about 165 lb (75 kg), but the world's heaviest dog was an English mastiff named Aicama Zorba. He tipped the scales at 343 lb (155 kg).

Although the average height of an adult male varies across the world, a rough average is 6 ft (1.8 m).

5¾ ft (1.75 m)

5 ft (1.5 m)

4 ft (1.25 m)

3¼ ft (1 m)

1½ ft
(0.5 m)

¾ ft
(0.25 m)

If Zeus stood up
on his hind legs,
he could reach
7¼ ft (2.24 m) tall.

Zeus
the Great Dane
is seven times
the height of
the smallest
dog breed.

**Chihuahuas are the
smallest dogs,** standing
6–9 in (15–23 cm) tall.

FAST FACTS

Longest dog ears
13½ in (34.3 cm)

The smallest dog ever was
a female chihuahua named
Heaven Sent Brandy. She
was less than half the
length of the longest
ears on a dog.

Smallest dog length
6 in (15.2 cm)

THUMBELINA

The world's smallest horse
is a dwarf miniature named
Thumbelina. At 17 in (43 cm)
tall, she's about the height of
a cocker spaniel and weighs
only 57 lb (26 kg).

What's the biggest jellyfish?

Jellyfish are **marine creatures** with **small bodies**, but some have incredibly **long tentacles**. The **lion's mane jellyfish** has tentacles **120 ft** (36.5 m) long!

Jellyfish tentacles contain venomous stinging cells, used for self-defense or to catch prey such as fish and shrimp.

The tentacles of the lion's mane jellyfish are arranged in eight groups of up to 150, so a single jellyfish could have 1,200 tentacles. This type of jellyfish is only ½ in (1 cm) at birth, but grows up to 230 times bigger. Its life expectancy is one year.

It would take more than 40 scuba divers in a line to be the same length as the tentacles of the lion's mane jellyfish.

The tentacles of a lion's mane jellyfish are as long as 2½ blue whales.

MOVING JELLY

Jellyfish have a nervous system, but no brain or eyes. They have three parts—the tentacles, bell, and oral arms. The bell is the pulsating jellylike body, which propels the jellyfish through water. Oral arms are used to direct food into the mouth opening.

The largest lion's mane jellyfish had a bell—or body—7½ ft (2.3 m) wide.

A blue whale is a whopping 100 ft (30 m) in length.

FAST FACTS

Larger lion's mane jellyfish are darker than small ones. The smallest are cream or orange, and the biggest are deep red or purple.

The biggest lion's mane jellyfish can weigh 1.1 tons (1 metric ton), which is heavier than a polar bear.

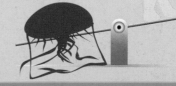

How **long** can **animals** hold their breath in **water?**

DEEP BREATH

In the extreme sport of free diving, divers use no breathing equipment but hold their breath as they sink deep underwater.

Many **air-breathing animals** can hold their breath for **hours** underwater: the loggerhead turtle manages **7 hours** (420 minutes). Some animals dive to **find food**, while others stay underwater to **sleep**.

Scuba divers can reach depths of 32 ft (10 m) for an hour if they have an adequate oxygen supply in the tank.

An average human can hold her breath for 30 seconds to 2 minutes; but the world record is 22 minutes. Do not try this at home!

SCUBA DIVER

ORCA

EMPEROR PENGUIN

HUMAN

1 minute

20 minutes

27 minutes

60 minutes

FAST FACTS

Whales breathe through blowholes, spraying water in shapes that can be used to identify their species.

Blue

Humpback

Southern right

Sperm

Free diver Herbert Nitsch held his breath while sinking to record-breaking depths of 830 ft (253 m). The deepest scuba dive was by Ahmed Gabr, reaching 1,090 ft (332 m).

Loggerhead turtles dive to find prey such as crabs and sponges, and to escape predators, including sharks and orcas. They come to the surface to breathe in short bursts just 1–3 seconds long.

A human would need **7 scuba tanks** to stay underwater as long as a loggerhead turtle.

A Cuvier's beaked whale was recorded underwater for 138 minutes. This species of whale dives deeper than any other, with one tracked to 9,816 ft (2,992 m).

LOGGERHEAD TURTLE

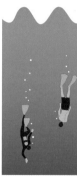

CUVIER BEAKED WHALE

AMERICAN ALLIGATOR

ELEPHANT SEAL

120 minutes

120 minutes

138 minutes

420 minutes

How tall is a termite mound?

The **largest nests** of any insect, termite mounds can reach **41 ft (12.5 m) above ground and 40 ft (12 m) in diameter**. It can take **five years** to build the mounds, with **termites burrowing up to 225 ft (70 m) underground.**

Taipei Tower, Taiwan
1,670 ft (509 m)

Completed in 2004, this skyscraper is Taiwan's financial center, standing 101 stories high.

Empire State Building, New York City, USA
1,453 ft (443 m)

Opened in 1931, this landmark building has 102 stories and an observation deck.

If people built to the same scale as a termite, the structure would be 2,000 ft (610 m) tall.

The Shard,
London, UK
1,016 ft (310 m)

Great Pyramid,
Giza, Egypt
481 ft (147 m)

Human

Termite

Shafts and tunnels in the mound help ventilate the soil and the underground nest, keeping the temperature at a comfortable level.

The mound is as hard as concrete. It is made of sand or clay held together with fibers of chewed wood and the termites' own saliva and waste. The nest continues underground, with tunnels spreading out more than 330 ft (100 m) wide.

Termites

Fungus

Termites need fungus to help them digest the wood they eat. The fungus farmed inside the mound takes up eight times more space than the termites do.

FAST FACTS

About 1–2 million termites live in a mound. Together they weigh about 33 lb (15 kg), but they can shift 550 lb (250 kg) of soil a year.

33 lb

A queen termite can be 30 times bigger than the workers. When pregnant, she grows to 4 in (10 cm). She lays an egg every three seconds for 15 years. Some queens live for 50 years, making them the world's oldest insects.

Worker

Queen

North America

The size of the swarm was estimated to be 1,800 miles (2,900 km) long and 110 miles (175 km) wide.

By eating their body-weight— 0.07 oz (2 g)— in vegetation a day, the locusts caused $200 million-worth of damage to crops between 1873 and 1877. This would be $4 billion today.

The biggest locust swarm attacked an area covered today by 11 US states.

FAST FACTS

There are 13 desert locusts for every person on Earth. They form today's biggest swarms, up to 460 sq miles (1,200 km²) in area.

Red-billed quelea form the biggest bird flocks. Numbers on the African plains can reach 10 billion.

One megacolony of Argentine ants stretches 3,700 miles (6,000 km) along Europe's Mediterranean coast.

How **big** is a **locust** swarm?

In 1875, **12.5 trillion** Rocky Mountain locusts descended on an area of **198,000 sq miles** (513,000 km²) in the western US.

North America

The density of locusts in this biggest-ever swarm led a witness to report that their "bodies hid the Sun and made darkness."

EXTINCT SPECIES

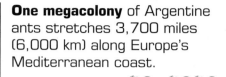

Fast wings for flight

Strong legs for jumping

Native to North America, the Rocky Mountain grasshopper (*Melanoplus spretus*) that swarmed in 1875 had died out by 1903.

How much **water** can an **elephant** hold in its **trunk?**

A large, male **African elephant** can suck up around **2½ gallons** (10 liters) of water in its trunk.

The two fingerlike projections at the end of the trunk are delicate and agile enough to pick up a peanut.

FAST FACTS

An elephant's trunk is up to 7 ft (2.1 m) long. With head raised and trunk extended, an elephant can reach up 23 ft (7 m) to pluck branches from trees.

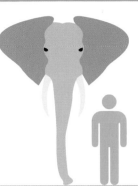

A trunk has five times the amount of smell receptors that are in a person's nose and can smell a banana from 165 ft (50 m) away.

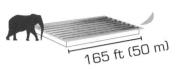

165 ft (50 m)

The trunk is strong enough to lift 770 lb (350 kg), the same weight as 28 gold bars.

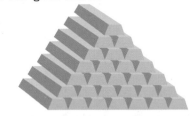

An elephant sucks up water in its trunk to drink, to spray clean its mouth, or to shower itself. Elephants also spray themselves with mud and dust to keep cool.

The trunk can weigh 400 lb (180 kg)—up to a quarter of the animal's total body weight.

An African elephant's trunk can hold as much liquid as 30 soda cans.

African elephants feed regularly. They use their trunks to tear off tough vegetation from trees before their large teeth break it down. Male elephants also fight for supremacy and females by wrestling with their trunks.

How big is a hippo's mouth?

A hippopotamus has a **very big** mouth, which can open to almost **180 degrees**. This creates an enormous **gape** of **4 ft** (1.2 m).

The name "hippopotamus" means "water horse," and most of this animal's time is spent in Africa's rivers and water holes. Its eyes have a protective membrane, which allows it to see underwater, and it can stay submerged without breathing for at least five minutes.

DISPLAY OF AGGRESSION

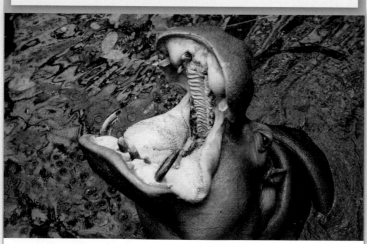

Hippos are the most dangerous large animal in Africa, killing 300 people a year. An open mouth is a sign of aggression, displaying canine teeth (tusks) up to 19 in (50 cm) long.

The jaw can open so wide because the jaw hinge is set far back in the head.

A hippo's jaw opens wide enough to fit a **sports car** inside.

The height of a **Ferrari Modena** car is 4 ft (1.2 m)—about as tall as a seven-year-old child.

The **mouth opens** wide when rival males are fighting or females are protecting their young.

📊 FAST FACTS

The biggest mouth of any animal belongs to the bowhead whale. The official world record is 16 ft (5 m) long, 8 ft (2.5 m) wide, and 12 ft (4 m) tall—three times bigger than a hippo's mouth.

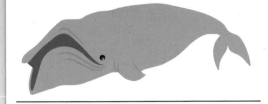

The longest tongue relative to body size belongs to the tube-lipped bat. At 3½ in (85 mm) long, the tongue is 1.5 times the bat's body length and is extended into the tube flowers on which it feeds. When the bat is not feeding, the tongue retracts into the rib cage.

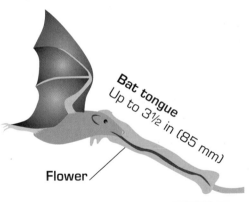

Bat tongue
Up to 3½ in (85 mm)

Flower

A woodpecker's tongue can be up to three times the length of its beak. The tongue curls up around its skull when not in use. The bird hammers its beak against trees, making holes for the tongue to probe inside the trunk for insects.

Tongue
Up to 6¾ in (170 mm)

What's the **ocean's deadliest animal?**

Many sea creatures deliver a **painful bite**, while others give a **deadly sting**. The deadliest of them all is the dreaded **box jellyfish**.

A box jellyfish has around 60 tentacles, each containing around 5,000 stinging cells.

World's most venomous fish, but deaths are rare

Stonefish

Fewer than 10 people per year die from shark attacks

Great white shark

About 150 people a year are thought to die from sea snake bites, but not all bites are lethal

Sea snake

From 2000 to 2015, 290 people died from "saltie" attacks

Saltwater crocodile

Just 1 oz (30 g) of **box jellyfish** venom can kill **60 people** in **three minutes**.

Box jellyfish

📊 FAST FACTS

Box jellyfish venom is so powerful it can stop a human heart in seconds. These jellyfish have killed more than 5,500 people since 1954, which would fill an Airbus A380 passenger plane more than six times.

Airbus A380 carries 853 people per plane

STINGER SCARS

This picture shows the scars left from a jellyfish sting on human skin. Fortunately, the sting was treated and did not cause a painful death.

What's the most indestructible animal?

Tardigrades, also called water bears, are classed as **extremophiles:** creatures that can **adapt and survive** in the **harshest** conditions.

Tardigrades are about 0.02 in (0.5 mm) long.

In extreme environments, a tardigrade sheds more than 95 percent of its body water and shrivels into a blob, called a tun.

Tardigrades can survive more than 285 times the radiation a human can stand.

5,700 gray (Gy)

BORN SURVIVORS

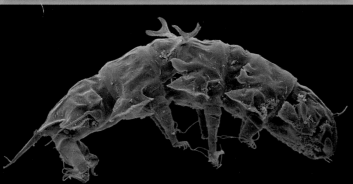

This close-up of a tardigrade shows it has tiny claws at the end of its four pairs of stumpy legs. It is a tiny animal that lives in moisture, using its claws to clamber through moss, soil, or sand.

Tough tardigrades have survived in many extreme environments:

Existing in the vacuum of space for 10 days. A human can last only two minutes.

Freezing at -458 °F (-272 °C).

Heating to more than 300 °F (150 °C).

Pressure 6,000 times that of the deepest part of the ocean.

Tardigrades are almost impossible to kill. They can take in huge levels of radiation, measured in Gray (Gy), that would kill off any other creature. They first appeared more than 600 million years ago and have survived all five mass extinction events in Earth's history.

The Habrobracon wasp is a resilient insect, able to withstand 90 times more radiation than a human can.

Hardy cockroaches can survive for a few weeks without their heads.

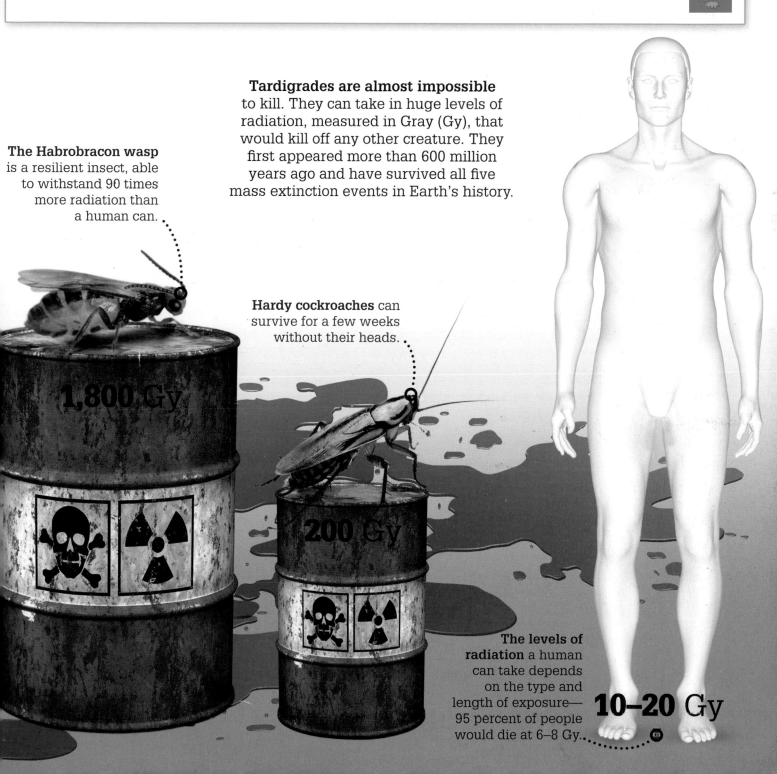

1,800 Gy

200 Gy

The levels of radiation a human can take depends on the type and length of exposure— 95 percent of people would die at 6–8 Gy.

10–20 Gy

In 2015, **a blue whale** washed up in Newfoundland, Canada, was the first to have its heart fully preserved for scientific study. The whale was 78 ft (24 m) long.

A blue whale's heart weighs as much a motorcycle.

The Honda CBR600FS weighs around 400 lb (180 kg) without fuel.

The aorta, or main artery, is so wide, a human head can fit inside.

BEACHED WHALE

Very occasionally, a blue whale carcass gets washed up on the beach. Its huge size increases as it decomposes and gets filled with methane gas, which can make it explode.

The heart and arteries are huge to allow enough blood through to reach all areas of the whale's 100-ft (30-m) long body.

How **heavy** is a blue whale's **heart?**

The world's largest animal comes with a supersized **heart** that weighs **400 lb** (180 kg) and pumps **11 tons** (10 metric tons) of **blood** around the whale's body.

ENTRANCE HOLES

A sociable weaver's nest is dotted with entrance holes for the birds to access their own chamber within the nest. Straw is positioned in spikes around the holes to keep invaders out.

Nests are usually built in the safety of trees with high branches to avoid predators.

Which **bird** builds the **largest** nests?

The **sociable weaver** of southern Africa constructs the **largest** nests of any bird, building one giant nest for the **entire colony**. These intricate structures can be **13 ft** (4 m) in height.

Sociable weaver birds fill trees with nests large enough to house up to 400 birds.

Grass and twigs are the main building materials.

Weaver birds live in the Kalahari Desert. Their nests are constructed so that the bottom part stays cool, providing respite from the desert heat.

The nest contains multiple entrances, measuring 10 in (25 cm) long and 3 in (7 cm) wide.

📊 FAST FACTS

A pair of bald eagles built the single largest bird nest. Created in 1963 in Florida, it was 9½ ft (2.9 m) wide and 20 ft (6 m) deep. That's big enough to fit a car inside!

Malleefowl birds lay eggs in mounds made of leaf-litter and bark. The eggs are covered in sand for warmth. The biggest known mound was 15 ft (4.6 m) tall and 35 ft (10.6 m) wide.

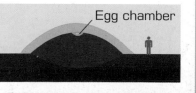

Egg chamber

Animal data

LUMINOUS ANIMALS

▶ Many **scorpions** are **fluorescent**—they have molecules on their body surface that glow in ultraviolet light

▶ When attacked, **Atolla jellyfish** emit a brilliant **burst of light** that can be seen up to **300 ft** (91 m) away.

▶ **Comb jellies** produce **blue** or green **light**, but moving their body can scatter the light to create multicolored moving patterns.

▶ Some **click beetles** emit a **bright light** to ward off predators; their light is so strong that you can read by it.

▶ **Railroad worms** are a form of glow-worm (beetle larva) that can give off **light in different** colors; their head glows red, while the body has green spots.

▶ **Sea sparkles** (*Noctiluca scintillans*) are tiny sea creatures that form huge colonies up to 80 miles (128 km) long. When disturbed, they flash **blue-green phosphorescent light** across miles of ocean.

UNUSUAL EYES

• The **chiton mollusk** has **more eyes than any other animal**. Embedded in its shell are thousands of eyes made of minerals, which can see light and shapes.

• The **tuatara lizard** has a so-called "**third eye**" on the top of its head, which **detects changes in light.**

• **Starfish** have basic **eye spots** at the **end of each arm** that can make out **light** and **large shapes**. Blue stars can see to a distance of **3 ft** (1 m), and each eye spot has a **170–220 degree** field of vision—slightly wider than that of a human.

• **Mexican tetra** fish species includes a blind variety that **lives in caves**. The lack of eyes means the **blind fish use 15 percent less energy** than the sighted ones.

NEEDLEWORK NEST

Tailorbirds curl up leaves to build nests inside. They make **tiny holes** along the edge of the leaf and use **plant fibers** or even **spider webs** to **stitch** the leaf in place.

BLOOD COLORS

Not all **blood** is **red**.

Crabs have blue blood.

Earthworms and **leeches** have green blood.

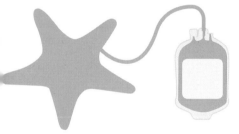

Many invertebrates, such as **starfish**, have clear or yellowish blood.

ELECTRICITY GENERATORS

▶ **Platypuses** have electrical receptors in their snouts to detect prey animals.

▶ **Stargazer fish** shoot electric currents from their eyes to stun their prey or drive away predators.

▶ **Electric rays** can set their electric impulses to different settings. They use a mild pulse to ward off aggressors. To attack prey, they use the full setting of up to 220V—double that of an electrical appliance in your home.

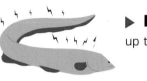

▶ **Electric eels** can give off a charge of up to 650V—strong enough to kill people.

FASTEST AND SLOWEST HEARTBEATS

• A **blue whale's** heart beats at **6 beats per minute (bpm)**, while a **hummingbird's** heart beats at up to **1,260 bpm**.

1,260 bpm

6 bpm

SMARTEST ANIMALS

• **Ants** are skillful farmers. They cultivate "gardens" of fungi and keep aphids for the sweet honeydew they produce.

• **Crows** can solve complex problems and make tools from sticks and wire to help them reach food. Some are better at problem-solving than a 5-year-old child.

• **Octopuses** have 130 million nerve cells, 60 percent of which are in their arms. They can play with toys, solve puzzles, and even learn their own names.

• **Bees** carry a mental map of flowers up to 3 miles (5 km) away from their hive. They perform "waggle dances" to tell other bees where to go. The duration of the dance indicates the distance to food, while the angle shows the direction.

How **big** can a **snail** grow?

Although they have a reputation for being **slow**, snails are not always **small**. Meet the **giant Ghana snail**, the world's **largest** land snail. This creature's **shell** can grow to an incredible **12 in** (30 cm) long and **6 in** (15 cm) wide.

An eye is situated at the tip of each tentacle.

SPIRAL SANCTUARY

Snails are part of a group of mollusks called gastropods. Not all have shells, but those that do usually have spiral-shaped shells that the creatures hide inside, away from predators.

FAST FACTS

One mighty marine snail boasts an even bigger shell. The Australian trumpet snail has a shell three times longer than the giant Ghana snail; the shell weighs as much as a three-year-old child.

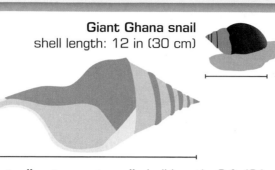

Giant Ghana snail
shell length: 12 in (30 cm)

Australian trumpet snail shell length: 3 ft (91 cm)

The biggest land snail was Gee Geronimo. At 15½ in (39.3 cm), its body was longer than a Dachshund.

Giant Ghana snails are native to several west African countries, not just Ghana. The average giant snail grows to around 8 in (20 cm) long and 4 in (10 cm) wide, but larger individuals can grow to 150 percent that size.

The striped shell gives the snail its other common name of giant tiger snail.

A giant Ghana snail is **longer than** a child's **open palms** put together.

How many eggs do animals lay?

Midwife toads are experts at taking care of eggs. Once the female lays her eggs, the male carries them on his back legs until hatching time, when he deposits them in ponds.

A **chicken** lays **an egg a day**, but that's nothing compared to other creatures in the animal kingdom. **Fish** and **insects** tend to be the most prolific producers, especially the **African driver ant**, which can lay up to **4 million eggs** every 25 days.

On average, chickens lay 260 eggs a year, so there are days when they don't lay.

Most snakes lay pale eggs with leathery shells.

Smaller sharks lay eggs in rubbery pouches known as "mermaid's purses."

Chicken
1 EGG

Brownbanded bamboo shark
2 EGGS

Cape cobra
20 EGGS

Hawksbill turtle
200 EGGS

FAST FACTS

The smallest eggs in the animal kingdom are laid by a fly called *Clemelis pullata*. The eggs are 0.0007 in x 0.001 in (0.02 mm x 0.02 mm).

You could line up 100 fly eggs across the width of this oval

Carpenter bees lay the largest insect eggs. The biggest ever found were ⅔ in (16.5 mm) long and 0.1 in (3 mm) across.

Carpenter bee and egg

Ostriches lay the most bird eggs in one nest. Up to 74 eggs can be in one nest, laid by all the females in the flock. An egg is laid every 2–3 days.

The eggs shown here are sized in relation to their mother animal. The numbers refer to the amounts laid at one time—a period that could be moments during one day or constant laying over many days.

The **African driver ant queen lays hundreds of thousands of eggs in a day.**

The gender of turtles young depends on the temperature of the eggs at incubation. Up to 82 °F (28 °C) produces males, while over 32 °C (90 °F) produces females. Temperatures in between produce males or females.

A queen honey bee lays 200,000 eggs every year of her life, which can be up to 8 years.

In a lifetime, the gray grouper produces about 300 million eggs, with some spawning 200,000 at once.

Honey bee
2,000 EGGS

Gray grouper
200,000 EGGS

African driver ant
3–4 MILLION EGGS

What's the smallest living reptile?

The miniature chameleon species ***Brookesia micra*** was first discovered in **Madagascar** in **2014**. It is only **1 in** (29 mm) long from nose to tail.

Chameleons can change the color of their skin, depending on their mood. Spotted patterns appear when *Brookesia micra* is angry or stressed. This can also help them to merge with their surroundings and keep hidden from predators and prey.

Each eye can move independently, but also work together to track prey accurately.

FAST FACTS

The largest living reptile is the saltwater crocodile, which can reach a whopping 18 ft (5.5 m). This is the same length as lining up 190 mini chameleons.

Saltwater crocodile
18 ft (5.5 m)

Mini chameleon
1 in (29 mm)

The chameleon's tiny size and brown color are useful in keeping it hidden from predators as it wanders through leaf litter on the forest floor.

This **mini chameleon** is **small enough to fit on the end of a pencil.**

The tail wraps around branches for balance at night when the chameleon sleeps up in the trees.

TONGUE TRAP

Chameleons catch prey using their long, sticky tongue. The bearded pygmy chameleon's tongue is more than twice its body length of 3 in (8 cm). Some chameleons can fire their tongues at prey in one-hundredth of a second—1,000 times faster than a sports car can accelerate.

What's the most venomous snake?

The snake with the **most potent venom** is the **inland taipan**, native to Australia. Luckily, **attacks** are **rare** and have been **treated** successfully.

This snake's skin changes color with the seasons, turning lighter in summer and darker in winter.

Inland taipans can reach up to 8 ft (2.5 m) in length.

VENOMOUS STRIKE

Snakes kill small mammals by biting them and injecting venom through their hollow fangs. They can open their jaws wide enough to swallow prey whole.

One bite from an **inland taipan** contains enough **venom** to kill **100 adult men**.

Taipan snake venom contains potent neurotoxins, which are poisons that cause muscle weakness and paralysis.

FAST FACTS

Scientists estimate that the venom from an inland taipan could kill a person within 45 minutes.

The fangs of an inland taipan grow up to ¼ in (6.2 mm), but this is small compared to the snake with the longest fangs. The Gaboon viper's fangs can be 2 in (5 cm) long.

Gaboon viper

Life-size fangs

Taipan

There have been no recorded deaths from an inland taipan bite in Australia. In contrast, honey bees kill up to two people a year in Australia.

The bottles represent the number of people one bite could kill.

Despite also being known as the "fierce snake," the inland taipan is not aggressive. It lives in remote, semidesert regions, which are home to very few people.

How **big** can a **squid** grow?

The **largest** specimen of **giant squid** ever seen was **59 ft** (18 m) long and weighed in at a hefty **2,000 lb** (900 kg). They live in the depths of the oceans and are rarely seen.

The 59-ft (18-m) specimen is an unofficial record. Scientific studies put the squid's maximum length at 43 ft (13 m) from its mantle to its outstretched tentacles.

The mantle, or main body, covers the squid's internal organs, including its heart, stomach, and gills.

The eyes of the giant squid are the size of dinner plates. The only creature with bigger eyes is the colossal squid.

📊 FAST FACTS

A squid moves quickly by jet propulsion: it sucks water into its mantle, then pushes it out through its funnel. It uses its fins to move at slow speeds.

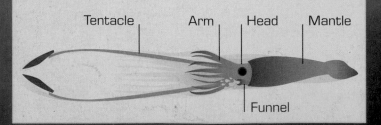

Tentacle   Arm   Head   Mantle

Funnel

LOOK AT THOSE SUCKERS

The squid's arms and tentacles have hundreds of rings of suckers. They are lined with teeth made from chitin, a similar substance to fingernails.

The squid has eight arms lined with suckers for gripping prey. It also has two tentacles, up to three times longer than its arms, used for pushing food into its mouth.

Three people can squeeze inside the 13-ft (4-m) long Triton 3300/3 submarine. It can explore down to 3,300 ft (1,000 m) deep.

The largest giant squid was 4.5 times longer than a Triton submarine.

How many bees make a jar of honey?

In its **lifetime**, an average bee will produce **one-twelfth** of a **teaspoon** of honey. It takes **800 bees**, collecting the nectar of **2 million** flowers, to make enough honey to fill **one jar**.

FAST FACTS

Earth

Bees fly 55,000 miles (88,500 km)—more than twice around the world— to produce one jar of honey.

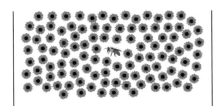

One honey bee visits up to 100 flowers in each flight, collecting nectar and pollen as food.

The world's most expensive honey comes from a cave 6,000 ft (1,800 m) deep in northeastern Turkey. Called Elvish honey, it sells for $2,500 per pound—more expensive than gold!

$2,500

A colony of honey bees is made up of a queen, up to 60,000 female worker bees, and hundreds of male, stingless drones.

Bee wings flap 230 times per second, creating a buzzing sound.

It takes **800 bees** to make enough **honey** to fill **a 1 lb (450 g) jar.**

Honey is the only food that never spoils. Perfectly preserved pots thousands of years old have been found in ancient Egyptian tombs.

POLLEN BASKETS

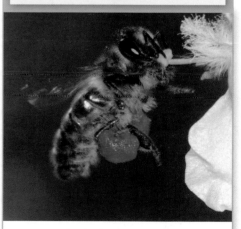

Bees feed on flower pollen and take it back to the hive for the colony. Using their middle legs, they brush pollen caught on their hairy body into "baskets" on their back legs.

What's the biggest rat?

The **Bosavi woolly rat** was discovered in **2009** in Papua New Guinea. This rodent measures **32 in** (82 cm) from head to tail, making it **twice the length** of a common rat.

An expedition team in the jungles of Papua New Guinea found this giant rat living high up in a volcano crater. It weighed 3¼ lb (1.5 kg), more than the combined weight of three common rats.

A child could just about **pick up** a Bosavi woolly rat in his or her **hands**.

RODENT RECORD

The capybara of South America is the biggest rodent of all, weighing up to 145 lb (66 kg)— the same as a person. Capybaras are mainly aquatic and feed on plants and grasses.

FAST FACTS

Fossils of ancient rats found in Southeast Asia revealed seven rat species the same size and weight as a small dog.

The fossilized rat bones are around twice the length of bones from a modern rat.

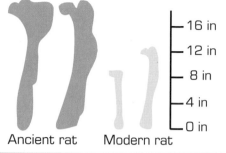

Ancient rat   Modern rat

16 in
12 in
8 in
4 in
0 in

The ancient rats weighed 11 lb (5 kg)—12 times more than an average common rat today.

A thick fur coat helps this rat to survive in the cool, damp mountain forest.

A long tail helps the rat to keep its balance as it walks along high ridges.

Rotor blades move at high speed, creating a loud whirring noise that can be heard up to 5 miles (8 km) away. At 100 ft (30 m) away, the noise reaches 100 dB.

EAR-SPLITTING SOUND

Humans can withstand 160 dB before sound levels split eardrums. A loud rock concert reaches 115 dB, while a jet engine gets up to 140 dB.

Unlike an aircraft, a helicopter can take off without a runway, move backward and sideways, and turn in midair.

How loud is an insect?

The **African cicada** (*Brevisana brevis*) is the world's **loudest insect**, with a call averaging **106.7 decibels (dB)** at a distance of **20 in** (50 cm) away.

FAST FACTS

The loudest noise in the animal kingdom is made by the tiger pistol shrimp. This is not a vocal sound, but the snapping of its claws. Blue whales also produce a loud noise, almost twice as loud as the African cicada's call.

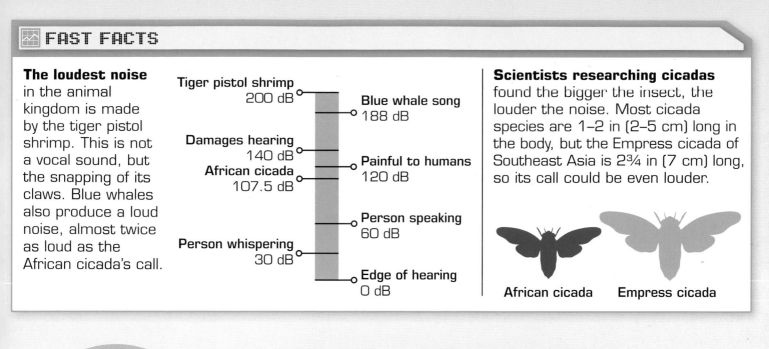

Tiger pistol shrimp
200 dB

Blue whale song
188 dB

Damages hearing
140 dB

Painful to humans
120 dB

African cicada
107.5 dB

Person speaking
60 dB

Person whispering
30 dB

Edge of hearing
0 dB

Scientists researching cicadas found the bigger the insect, the louder the noise. Most cicada species are 1–2 in (2–5 cm) long in the body, but the Empress cicada of Southeast Asia is 2¾ in (7 cm) long, so its call could be even louder.

African cicada   Empress cicada

The **African cicada's** call is **louder** than a helicopter.

Male cicadas make their deafening calls using two organs called tymbals, which are made up of a membrane stretched over ribs. The tymbal makes a clicking sound when the cicada contracts (squeezes) it and when it relaxes it. A cicada can produce 300–400 clicks every second.

Four transparent wings are folded up when the cicada is not in flight.

A male cicada has a tymbal on each side of its abdomen. The clicking sound is amplified (made louder) by the insect's hollow body.

ANCIENT GIANTS

Prehistoric invertebrates (animals without a backbone), such as this millipede, grew to giant sizes because there was more oxygen in the atmosphere at the time. This enabled the bugs' body tissues to grow large. The bugs began to shrink when oxygen levels fell.

Compound eyes (eyes made up of many parts) provided multiple images, helping the insect detect movement and judge distances with amazing accuracy. ....

Biting jaws tore into ancient prey, including small reptiles and amphibians.

What was the **biggest insect** ever?

The **prehistoric griffenfly** *Meganeuropsis permiana* was about **17 in** (43 cm) long. This insect was the **ancestor** of today's **dragonflies** and damselflies.

The abdomen may have been brightly colored like that of a modern dragonfly. The color makes the males more attractive to females.

The length of *Meganeuropsis permiana's* body was **twice the diameter** of a soccer ball.

With a wingspan of 28 in (71 cm), this insect could wrap its wings around a soccer ball. It was able to fly backward and upside down and reached top speeds of 35 mph (56 kph).

A soccer ball has a diameter of about 9 in (22 cm)—half the length of this insect's body.

FAST FACTS

Dragonflies and damselflies have evolved to be much smaller than their distant ancestors. Today's largest damselfly has a wingspan of 7½ in (19 cm)—just over a quarter of the size of the prehistoric species.

Largest modern damselfly:
Megaloprepus caerulatus

Largest known insect:
Meganeuropsis permiana

Meganeuropsis permiana was the length of an eagle but weighed the same as a crow: 1 lb (450 g).

What's the smallest insect?

The **smallest**, fully grown adult **insect** is a **male fairyfly** (a parasitic wasp) of the species *Dicopomorpha echmepterygis*. These blind, wingless insects are only **0.005 in** (0.139 mm long.

ESSENTIAL EGGS

The fairyfly is a parasite that lives in the egg of a bark louse (shown above). The male fairyfly dies in the egg, but the female chews her way out so she can lay her own eggs in other hosts before she dies.

A typical grain of rice is 1/8 in (4 mm) long and 0.1 in (2.5 mm) wide.

Parasitic wasps have no stinger and are completely harmless to people. There are hundreds of different varieties: most are tiny in size and brown or black in color. They have two pairs of wings and long antennae.

FAST FACTS

The male wasp is just one-eighth the size of the female (by volume). Females range in length from 0.015 in to 0.022 in (0.39 mm to 0.55 mm).

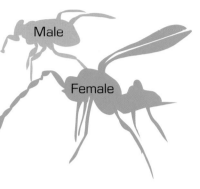

Male

Female

Some of the tiniest animals of all are lociferans, which live between grains of sand. At 0.0004 in (0.01 mm) long, the smallest lociferan is 200 times smaller than a grain of sand.

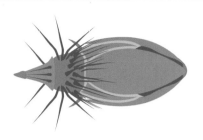

Shown at 4,500 times its real size

Male fairyflies use their antennae to search for a mate.

A line of **29 male** *Dicopomorpha echmepterygis* **fairyflies** could fit on a **grain of rice**.

Rice is the seed of a species of grass, and comes in 40,000 different varieties.

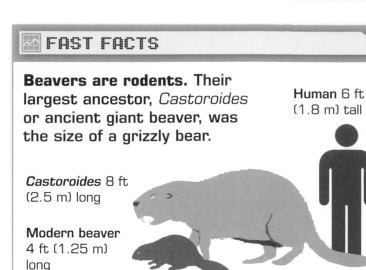

Beavers are rodents. Their largest ancestor, *Castoroides* or ancient giant beaver, was the size of a grizzly bear.

Human 6 ft (1.8 m) tall

Castoroides 8 ft (2.5 m) long

Modern beaver 4 ft (1.25 m) long

The beaver dam is wider than two Hoover Dams.

The Hoover Dam is 1,205 ft (367 m) wide at the top.

Water makes turbines spin, creating hydroelectric power. The more water, the more energy is produced.

The Hoover Dam contains 17 generators that produce in excess of four billion kilowatt hours of electricity every year.

How big can beaver dams get?

One of the largest structures ever built by animals is a **beaver dam** in Alberta, Canada. It contains two beaver lodges and measures **2,800 ft** (850 m) **wide**.

The beaver dam is built of trees, mud, and stones, and is entered by an underwater opening.

Beavers build dams to create a pool of slow-moving water, in which they can then build their lodges (homes). The pool acts as protection from predators such as coyotes, and is also a source of food during winter.

The enormous construction was worked on by several families of beavers.

HIDDEN HOME

The record-breaking dam in a remote part of Canada is so big it can be seen from the Moon. In this satellite image, some of the dam (in brown) can been seen through the dense vegetation.

The concrete arch structure is 725 ft (221 m) high and 659 ft (201 m) thick, with 120 million cubic feet (3.4 million m³) of concrete used during its construction.

Which animal sleeps the most?

All **animals** need **sleep,** but how much **varies widely. Captive** animals **sleep longer** than those in the **wild**. The biggest sleepyhead is the **python,** dozing for up to **18 hours** a day.

HALF ASLEEP

Most whales sleep by resting one half of their brains at a time. Sperm whales, however, nap fully, but for only 10—15 minutes at a time. They sleep vertically so they can breathe at the surface.

Sloths in the wild sleep for 9.6 hours, but this can double to 18 hours in captivity.

Asia

Giraffes can sleep standing up or sitting down.

Sloth

2 hours **Giraffe**

3–4 hours **Elephant**

9.6 hours

FAST FACTS

Humans spend up to a third of their lives asleep.

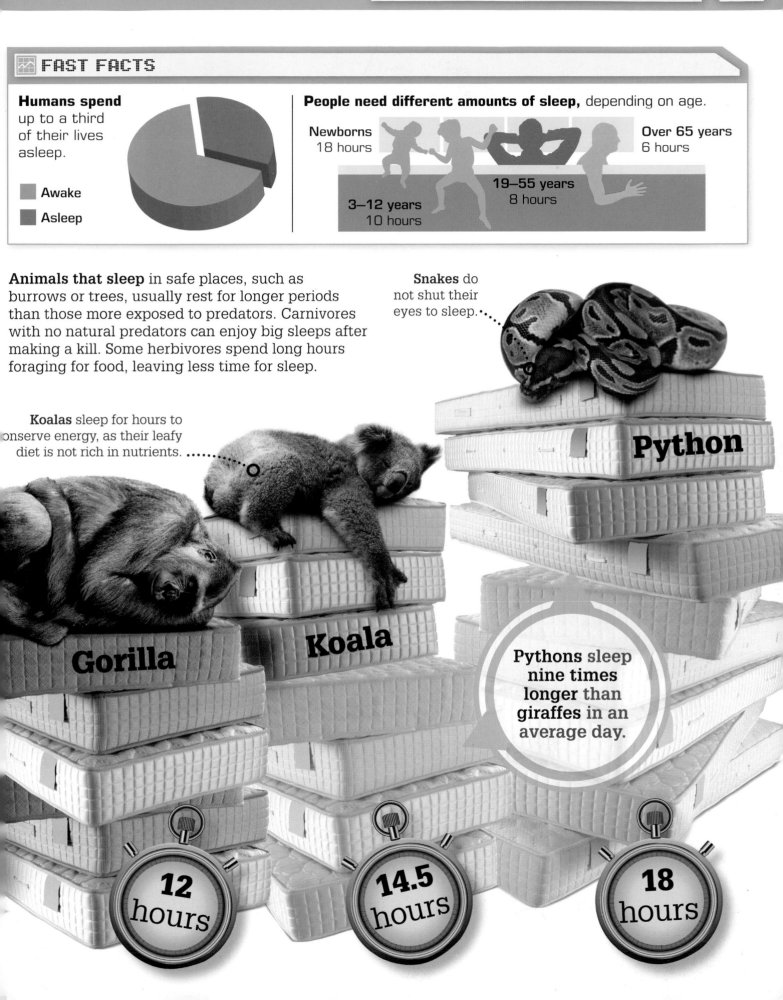

- Awake
- Asleep

People need different amounts of sleep, depending on age.

Newborns
18 hours

Over 65 years
6 hours

19–55 years
8 hours

3–12 years
10 hours

Animals that sleep in safe places, such as burrows or trees, usually rest for longer periods than those more exposed to predators. Carnivores with no natural predators can enjoy big sleeps after making a kill. Some herbivores spend long hours foraging for food, leaving less time for sleep.

Snakes do not shut their eyes to sleep.

Koalas sleep for hours to conserve energy, as their leafy diet is not rich in nutrients.

Python

Gorilla

Koala

Pythons sleep nine times longer than giraffes in an average day.

12 hours

14.5 hours

18 hours

How much wool do sheep produce?

Every year, the world's **one billion sheep** give us **2.2 million tons** (2 million metric tons) of wool. This works out to **6,040 tons** (5,479 metric tons) a day, or **4.2 tons** (3.8 metric tons) a minute.

ALPACA WOOL

Not all wool comes from sheep. In South America there are four million alpacas, which have more than 20 natural colors of fleece. Local people dye the thick wool and handweave it into brightly colored clothing.

Enough wool is produced to make a sweater for the **Statue of Liberty** every **4 minutes.**

FAST FACTS

The world's most expensive wool comes from the vicuña, a South American relative of the camel. Prices can reach $400 per pound. In 2013, a German firm produced a limited set of vicuña wool socks, with a pair costing €860 ($980).

$980

The wool sheared from a single sheep makes one fleece. This can produce eight sweaters large enough for an adult. Half the world's wool supply comes from three countries—China, Australia, and New Zealand.

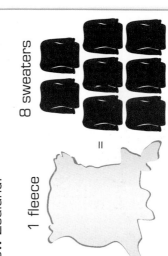

1 fleece = 8 sweaters

The sweater weighs 35½ lb (16.1 kg) and contains 105,610 ft (32,190 m) of yarn. This amount of yarn is produced every 4 minutes and 13 seconds across the world.

The statue's height from base to torch is 151 ft (46 m), making it the tallest iron structure in the world when it was built in 1886.

These sheep are shown life-size compared to the enormous scale of the Statue of Liberty.

Plant data

SEED SIZES

The **smallest** seeds come from species of tropical orchids, measuring just

85 micrometers

(¹/₃₀₀ in or 0.085 mm) **across**—invisible to the naked eye.

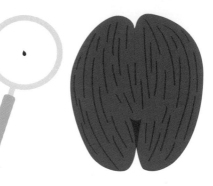

The **largest** and **heaviest** seeds of any plant are those of the coco de mer *(Lodoicea maldivica)*, which grows in the Seychelles islands. This palm seed can grow up to

20 in (50 cm)

across and weigh up to 55 lb (25 kg).

CARNIVOROUS PLANTS

▶ The **largest** known **carnivorous** plant, the giant montane pitcher plant of Borneo, has pitchers up to **2 quarts** (2 liters) **in volume**. These are big enough to hold a tree shrew. The plant eats the shrew's feces!

▶ **The Venus flytrap** snaps shut on prey in **0.3 seconds**, but it's not the fastest-moving carnivorous plant. Bladderworts are aquatic plants that trap their tiny prey in less than 1 millisecond: more than **100 times** faster than a Venus flytrap.

▶ The **pitcher plant** *Nepenthes attenboroughii*, which grows in the Philippines, has pitchers up to **12 in** (30 cm) tall—large enough to trap bigger insects and the occasional **small mammal**, such as shrews, to eat.

Giant montane pitcher plant

Venus flytrap

Nepenthes attenboroughii pitcher plant

L O N G E S T SEED "MIGRATIONS"

MOST POISONOUS PLANTS

- **The castor bean plant** produces castor oil, used in food, but the **seeds** also produce the **deadly poison ricin.** The ricin in just one bean *can kill an adult in minutes*.

- **Oleanders** are common garden plants, but they are also **highly toxic—just 0.14 oz (4 g) of oleander leaf** can deliver a dose of poison *lethal to humans*.

- **The rosary pea** has the **most potent poison** known to humanity. Despite the risks, the **red-and-black seeds** are often *made into jewelry*.

- **The manchineel,** which grows in Florida and central America, is the world's **most poisonous tree. All parts are toxic.** One drop of the sap can *cause burns on skin and strip paint off cars*.

EDIBLE AND MEDICINAL PLANTS

- There are about **80,000 known species of edible plant**—but we eat only about **150** of these species, and we get more than **90 percent** of our plant-based food from fewer than **20 species**. The top four are *rice*, *wheat*, *corn*, and *potatoes*.

- Around **50,000 plant species** have been used for medicinal purposes. One of the most widely used is **ginseng**. In Asia, its root has been used for more than **5,000** years to fight infection and increase energy.

The **Mary's bean** plant spreads its seeds by sea. One seed was recorded as drifting more than 15,000 miles (**24,000 km**) from the Wotho Atoll in the Pacific Ocean to Norway—the longest distance any seed has drifted.

FASTEST GROWING

Bamboos are the *fastest-growing of all plants.* Some species can grow up to **35 in** (91 cm) per day—or around **¹/₄ in** (3 cm) per hour.

The fastest-growing seaweed (actually a form of **algae**) is the **giant kelp**, which grows in the Pacific Ocean and the waters of South America, South Africa, and New Zealand. Its fronds can grow more than **148 ft** (45 m) tall, at a rate of up to **24 in** (60 cm) a day.

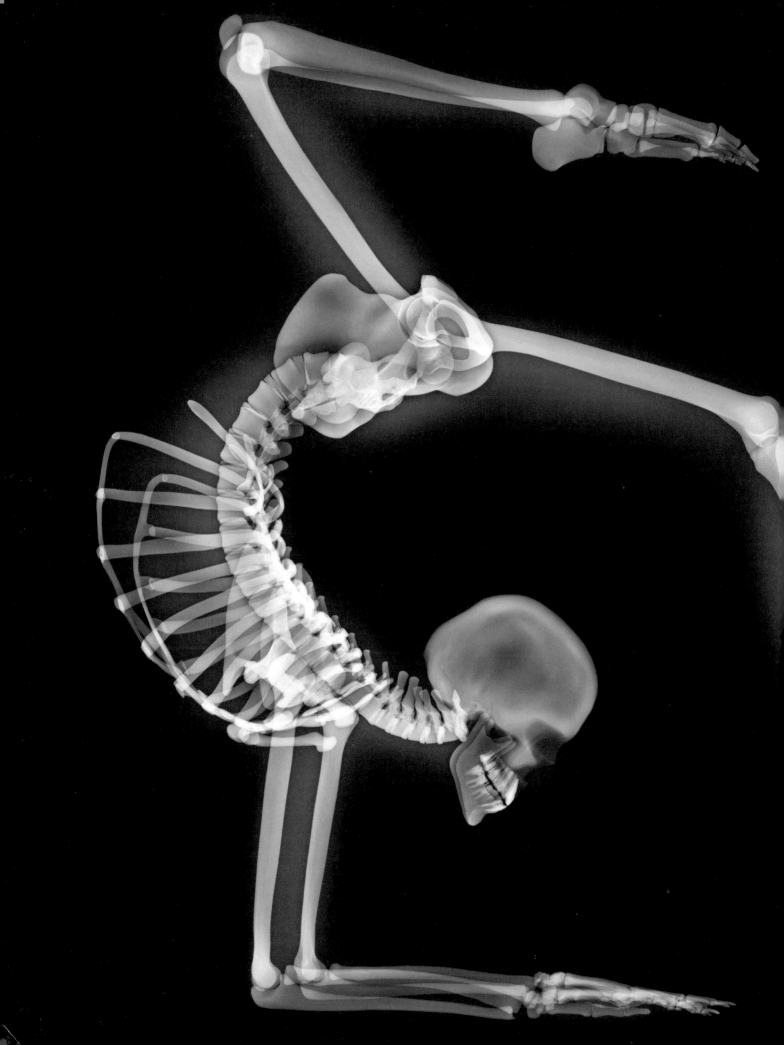

The human world

Many billions of people live and have lived on Earth, all of whom contribute to our rich ancestry. Though we all share the same living structure, each of us is one of a kind, with a unique combination of inherited genes, body cells, and personality traits.

The skeleton provides a supportive framework for the rest of the human body. Comprising 206 connected bones, it protects the vital organs. Muscles pull the bones to flex and move the body.

How many people live on Earth?

Our planet is home to **7.4 billion people**. If everyone stood next to each other, we could all fit into a **square** with **each side** measuring **21.8 miles** (35.11 km).

Kaua'i island covers an area of 554 sq miles (1,435 km²), with room for five people to stand in every square yard.

Everyone in the world could fit into the Hawaiian island of Kaua'i.

ASIAN POPULATION

More people live in Asia than in the rest of the world combined—about 4.4 billion people, or 60 percent of the population. China and India each have more than 1 billion residents.

The total area required to fit the entire global population is 476 sq miles (1,233 km²), which is slightly smaller than the Hawaiian island of Kaua'i in the Pacific Ocean.

Kaua'i

Hawaii

Hawaii's chain of six major islands includes Kaua'i, the oldest and most northerly island.

7,400,000,000 people

FAST FACTS

People around the world vary in height. The tallest live in the Netherlands, where the average man is 6 ft 1 in (184.8 cm) tall, while the shortest people are from Indonesia, with an average male standing 5 ft 2 in (157.5 cm) tall.

More people now live in cities than ever before. In 1960 most people lived in the countryside, with only 34 percent inhabiting urban areas. By 2014 about 54 percent of people lived in urban areas.

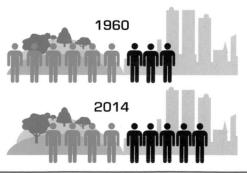

1960

2014

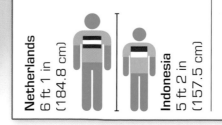

Netherlands
6 ft 1 in
(184.8 cm)

Indonesia
5 ft 2 in
(157.5 cm)

How long have people been on Earth?

Our species, *Homo sapiens*, emerged about **200,000 years ago**, but our *Homo* **ancestors** first appeared more than **2.4 million years ago** (mya). This is only **1.5 percent** of the time that **dinosaurs roamed Earth**.

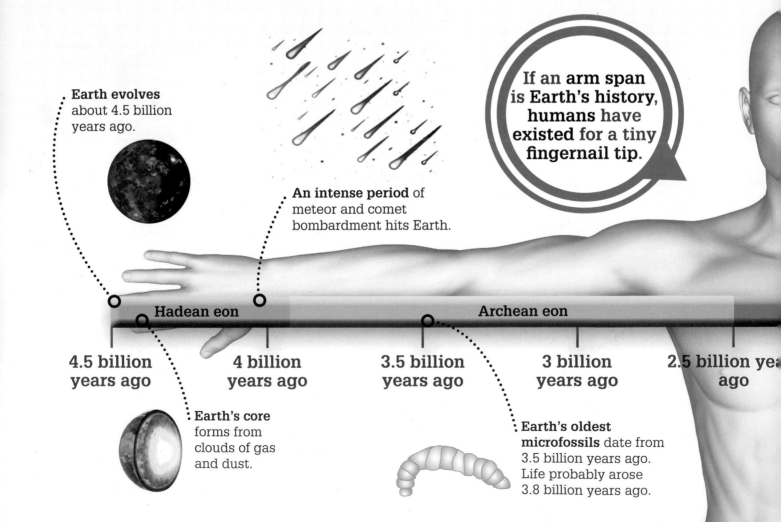

Earth evolves about 4.5 billion years ago.

An intense period of meteor and comet bombardment hits Earth.

If an **arm span** is Earth's history, **humans** have **existed** for a tiny **fingernail tip**.

Hadean eon

Archean eon

4.5 billion years ago

4 billion years ago

3.5 billion years ago

3 billion years ago

2.5 billion years ago

Earth's core forms from clouds of gas and dust.

Earth's oldest microfossils date from 3.5 billion years ago. Life probably arose 3.8 billion years ago.

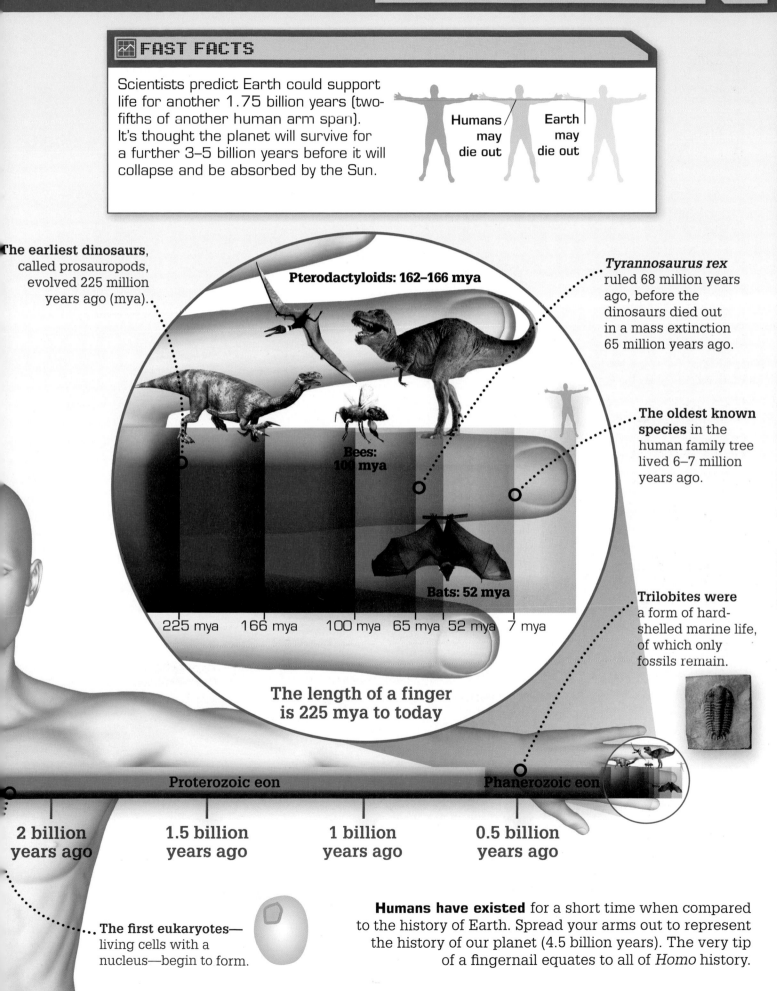

FAST FACTS

Scientists predict Earth could support life for another 1.75 billion years (two-fifths of another human arm span). It's thought the planet will survive for a further 3–5 billion years before it will collapse and be absorbed by the Sun.

Humans may die out

Earth may die out

The earliest dinosaurs, called prosauropods, evolved 225 million years ago (mya).

Pterodactyloids: 162–166 mya

Bees: 100 mya

Bats: 52 mya

225 mya   166 mya   100 mya   65 mya   52 mya   7 mya

The length of a finger is 225 mya to today

Tyrannosaurus rex ruled 68 million years ago, before the dinosaurs died out in a mass extinction 65 million years ago.

The oldest known species in the human family tree lived 6–7 million years ago.

Trilobites were a form of hard-shelled marine life, of which only fossils remain.

Proterozoic eon

Phanerozoic eon

2 billion years ago

1.5 billion years ago

1 billion years ago

0.5 billion years ago

The first eukaryotes— living cells with a nucleus—begin to form.

Humans have existed for a short time when compared to the history of Earth. Spread your arms out to represent the history of our planet (4.5 billion years). The very tip of a fingernail equates to all of *Homo* history.

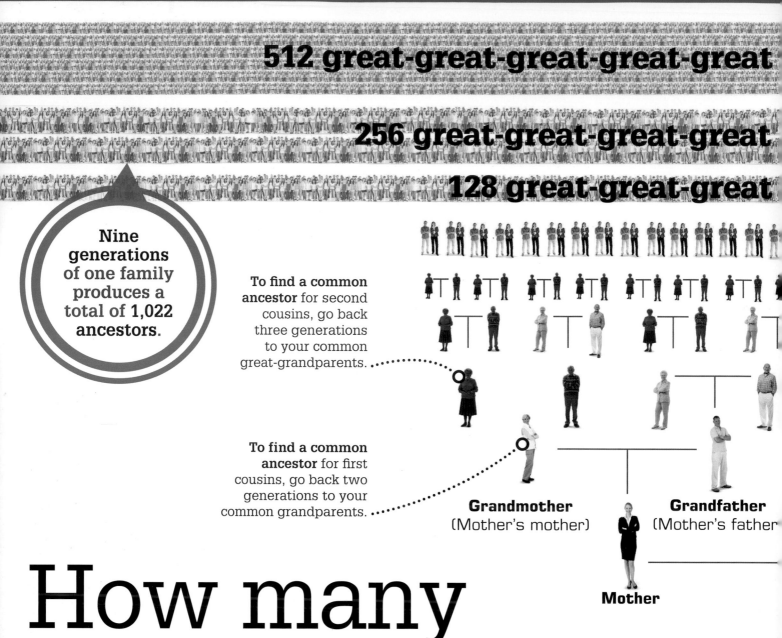

512 great-great-great-great-great

256 great-great-great-great

128 great-great-great

Nine generations of one family produces a total of **1,022** ancestors.

To find a common ancestor for second cousins, go back three generations to your common great-grandparents.

To find a common ancestor for first cousins, go back two generations to your common grandparents.

Grandmother
(Mother's mother)

Grandfather
(Mother's father)

Mother

How many ancestors do we have?

Your **family tree** starts with you today, but involves many thousands of other people making up **generations** of family **history**. Going back just **two centuries** gives you **1,022** ancestors.

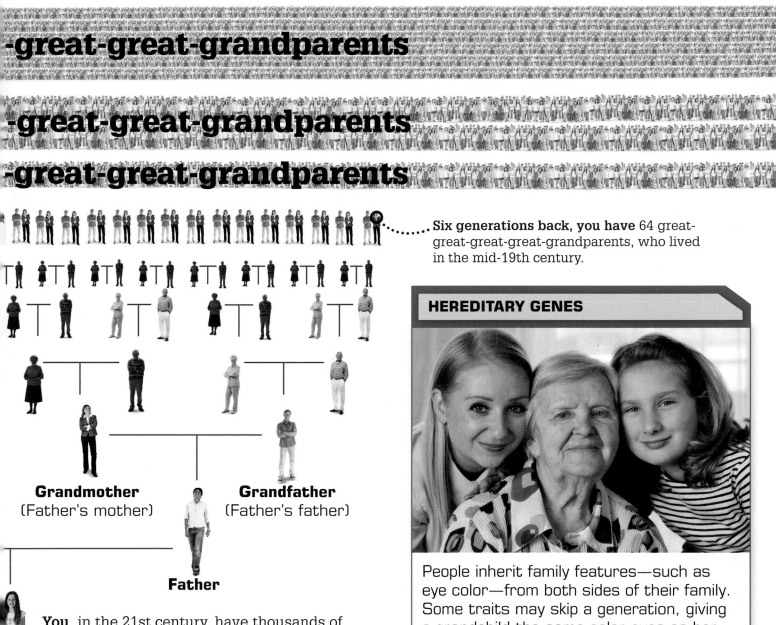

-great-great-grandparents

-great-great-grandparents

-great-great-grandparents

Six generations back, you have 64 great-great-great-great-grandparents, who lived in the mid-19th century.

Grandmother
(Father's mother)

Grandfather
(Father's father)

Father

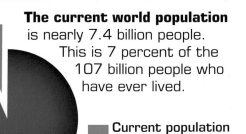

You, in the 21st century, have thousands of ancestors. Going back three centuries to the 12th generation gives you 8,190 ancestors. One generation is usually 20–25 years.

HEREDITARY GENES

People inherit family features—such as eye color—from both sides of their family. Some traits may skip a generation, giving a grandchild the same color eyes as her grandmother, but not her mother.

FAST FACTS

The current world population is nearly 7.4 billion people. This is 7 percent of the 107 billion people who have ever lived.

■ **Current population** 7.4 billion people

● **Total population** 107 billion people

Genghis Khan, Mongol leader in the 13th century, had many children. Today 8 percent of men in 16 Asian countries have genes suggesting they descended from him.

How **far** does a person **walk** in a **lifetime?**

The average person takes at least **5,000 steps** every day. Over a lifetime of 70 years, this adds up to a distance of more than **64,000 miles** (103,000 km).

FAST FACTS

Studies have shown that people of different nations walk different distances each day depending on their location and lifestyle.

It takes roughly 2,000 steps to cover a distance of 1 mile (1,240 steps over 1 km). Walking 5,000 steps a day covers 2.5 miles (4 km), but most people actually take more steps.

Average number of steps taken per day

- 12,000
- 10,000
- 8,000
- 6,000
- 4,000
- 2,000

USA | UK, Germany | Japan | Australia, Switzerland

THE WANDERER

The world's longest circumnavigation on foot was by Canadian Jean Béliveau. Starting in 2000, he walked through 64 countries in 11 years, covering 46,000 miles (75,000 km) and wearing out 54 pairs of shoes.

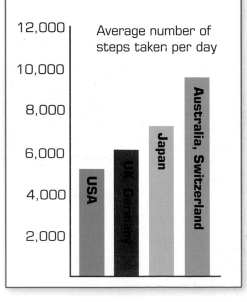

The equator is an imaginary line around Earth's center. At 24,902 miles (40,075 km) long, it would take almost 50 million steps to walk the length of it.

In **70 years**, the average person will walk **2.5 times** around Earth's **equator**.

Earth is not a perfect sphere— it is slightly squashed at the poles and bulges around the middle.

Time data

HAPPY BIRTHDAY

▶ In a group of **23 people**, there's more than a **50 percent** chance (actually 50.73 percent) that two of them share a birthday.

▶ With a group of **57 people**, there's a **99.01 percent** probability, and for **70 people** the probability is **99.92 percent.**

TIME IS MONEY

If you earned $1 every second, it would take 12 days to become a **millionaire,** but you would need 31 years to become a billionaire.

TIME IS RELATIVE

Einstein said that time changes depending on where you are (roughly speaking): the closer you are to the center of Earth, the slower time passes. If you were at the top of

Mount Everest,

a year would be 15 microseconds (millionths of a second) **shorter** than if you were at sea level.

Meanwhile, the shortest measure of time you can have is **Planck time**.
This is the time it takes for light to travel in a vacuum for a distance of 1 Planck length. This is the same as:

0.000,000,000,000,000,000,000,000, 000,000,000,000,000,000,054 seconds.

TIME ZONES

If everyone in the **world** set their **clocks** to noon, it would be **daytime** in some parts of the world and **nighttime** in others. To avoid this problem, **Earth** is divided into a number of **time zones**.

There are **39 different time zones** in use. Most are set whole hours ahead or behind GMT (Greenwich Mean Time). Some, however, are **30** or **45 minutes** different.

Greenwich, in London, UK, was chosen as the location of standard time because it lies at **0° longitude** on the world map.

Time zones meet at the **North** and **South Poles**. By walking around the poles, you can travel through **all** of the time zones in a few seconds.

India straddles **two** time zones, but has chosen a time halfway between them **(GMT + 5 h 30 m)** so that the whole country can use one time.

Time zones run along **lines of longitude**, but **bend** to include entire countries or states into one zone.

The Greenwich Meridian is an imaginary line that runs along **0° longitude.**

If you stood where the borders of Finland, Norway, and Russia meet, you can be in **three time zones at once!**

Russia has **11 time zones**—the most of any country.

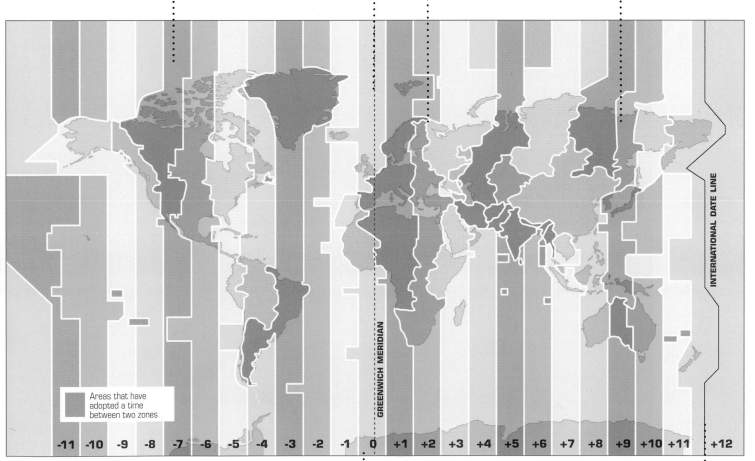

Areas that have adopted a time between two zones

GREENWICH MERIDIAN

INTERNATIONAL DATE LINE

-11   -10   -9   -8   -7   -6   -5   -4   -3   -2   -1   0   +1   +2   +3   +4   +5   +6   +7   +8   +9   +10   +11   +12

Each **time zone** is measured in hours ahead of or behind **GMT.** When it's **noon** in London, it's **1 p.m.** in most of Europe.

The **International Date Line** is an imaginary line at 180° longitude. Countries **east** of the line are one day **ahead** of those on the **west** of it.

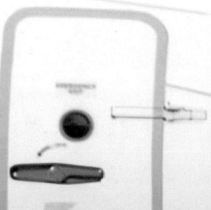

In 1990 Malaysian strong man Ramasamy Letchemanah used his hair to pull a Boeing 737 aircraft in Kuala Lumpur 56 ft (17 m), setting a new world record. His abilities were passed on to his daughter, who pulled a truck with her hair in 2002.

STICKY SITUATIONS

One head of hair pulled a 37 ton (34 metric tons) aircraft for a record-breaking 56 ft (17 m).

In some countries, hairdressers and pet groomers donate cut hair to help clean up oil spills at sea. Leaked oil clings to these hairy mats (above), just like oil coats your hair when it's on your head.

7 METER

8 METER

10 METER

11 METER

How strong is hair?

A **head** of **human hair** is strong enough to lift **13 tons** (12 metric tons). Just a small bunch of **100 hairs** can support **22 lb** (10 kg).

The Boeing 737 passenger aircraft weighed 37 tons (34 metric tons).

Letchemanah's hair was dressed in two braids to attach them to the aircraft.

Nicknamed "Mighty Man," Letchemanah went on to pull a double-decker bus in 1999.

FAST FACTS

Hair grows up to ½ in (1.25 cm) a month, or 6 in (15 cm) a year. Studies show Asian hair grows fastest, while African hair grows at nearer 4 in (10 cm) a year and Caucasian hair at 5 in (13 cm) a year.

It takes 2 years for hair to reach shoulder-length (10 in/25 cm)

It takes 7 years for hair to reach waist-length (34 in/85 cm)

12 METER   13 METER   14 METER   15 METER   16 METER   17 METER

How much power does your brain have?

Your brain has more than **80 billion neurons**, or nerve cells. When you're awake, these can generate **0.085 watts of electricity.**

Your brain generates enough **electricity** to power an **LED** lightbulb.

An average brain is about the size of a cauliflower. It is 75 percent water and has the texture of soft cheese.

The adult brain weighs about 3 lb (1.3 kg), which is only about two percent of the body's total weight—yet it uses 20 percent of the oxygen and 20 percent of the glucose in the blood.

Each groove on the brain's surface is called a sulcus, which means "furrow" in Latin. The ridged area around each sulcus is called a gyrus, which means "circle."

Electricity produced by the brain cannot be harnessed and used as a power supply. Rather, electrical signals carry messages within the brain and to the body. Billions of neurons act as messengers, carrying chemical and electrical signals between brain and body.

An LED (light-emitting diode) bulb is the most energy-efficient lightbulb, using 90 percent less energy than a traditional incandescent bulb.

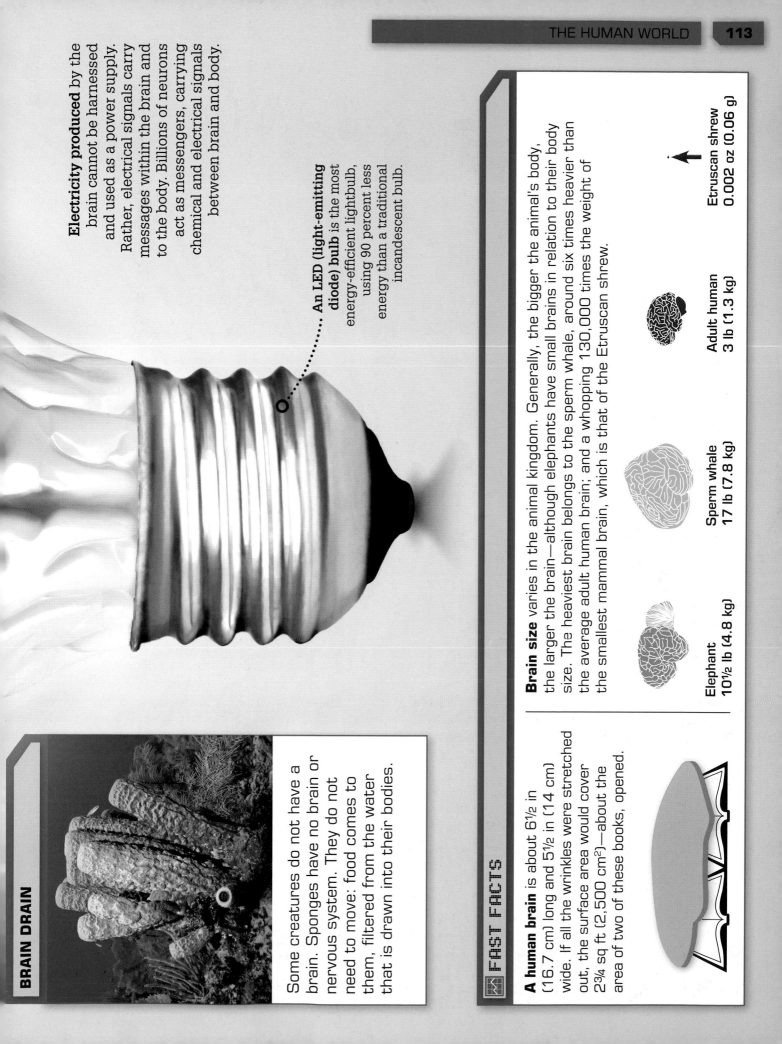

BRAIN DRAIN

Some creatures do not have a brain. Sponges have no brain or nervous system. They do not need to move: food comes to them, filtered from the water that is drawn into their bodies.

FAST FACTS

A human brain is about 6½ in (16.7 cm) long and 5½ in (14 cm) wide. If all the wrinkles were stretched out, the surface area would cover 2¾ sq ft (2,500 cm²)—about the area of two of these books, opened.

Brain size varies in the animal kingdom. Generally, the larger the animal's body, the bigger the animal's body. Generally, elephants have small brains in relation to their body size. The heaviest brain belongs to the sperm whale, around six times heavier than the average adult human brain; and a whopping 130,000 times the weight of the smallest mammal brain, which is that of the Etruscan shrew.

Elephant
10½ lb (4.8 kg)

Sperm whale
17 lb (7.8 kg)

Adult human
3 lb (1.3 kg)

Etruscan shrew
0.002 oz (0.06 g)

How much saliva do you produce in a day?

The **average person** produces between ½ and 1½ quarts (0.5–1.5 liters) of saliva a day, adding up to around **115 gallons** (436 liters) a year.

A **human** can produce enough spit **every day** to fill a 1½ quart (1.5 liter) bottle.

Saliva helps you dissolve substances in food in your mouth so they can come into contact with your taste buds, which detect tastes.

SALIVA!

SWIFT SALIVA

Many birds in the swift family use saliva to glue together nest materials. Some species make their nests from only saliva, which hardens in the air. These nests are used by people to make the delicacy bird's nest soup.

Saliva is produced by salivary glands. The three major pairs of salivary glands are located on the inside of each cheek, at the bottom of the mouth, and under the jaw at the front of the mouth.

Human saliva is 98 percent water, which helps to keep your mouth and teeth clean.

Helps to taste food!

Assists in keeping teeth clean!

1½ quarts
Contains water, electrolytes, enzymes, mucus, and bacteria-killing substances

The main purpose of saliva is to aid the body's digestive process. Food is moistened, making it easier to swallow; and broken down by substances called enzymes. Saliva is also a natural painkiller and mouth cleaner.

Most saliva is produced during the day, which is why people can wake up with dry mouths in the morning.

FAST FACTS

In a lifetime, a person creates enough saliva to fill between 1 and 2 large swimming pools.

Every time you cough, about 3,000 droplets of saliva are released from the mouth at speeds of up to 50 mph (80 kph).

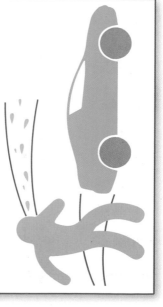

How much oxygen is in your body?

There are **25 different elements** in your body. **Oxygen** is by far the most abundant, at **65 percent** of your **body mass**. Adding **nitrogen, hydrogen, and carbon** accounts for **96 percent** of your mass.

Oxygen

This colorless gas allows your body cells to obtain the energy from food that keeps them alive.

Nitrogen

A small amount of nitrogen is needed to make complex molecules such as proteins and DNA.

All these elements are essential for life to exist. Elements are substances made from one type of atom; for example, oxygen is made of oxygen atoms. An atom is the smallest, most basic particle that cannot be broken down further. Atoms often bond with each other to produce molecules, such as water. Each water molecule contains two hydrogen atoms and one oxygen atom.

Hydrogen

These atoms are found inside important molecules such as fats, proteins, and carbohydrates.

Carbon

These atoms form the backbone of the complex molecules that make and run cells.

Two-thirds of your body is made up of oxygen.

Without the right elements, a body will not function properly. For example, calcium and phosphorus are needed to make strong bones and teeth.

FAST FACTS

Some 97.5 percent of body mass is made up of five elements. The other 2.5 percent includes phosphorus, potassium, sulfur, sodium, chlorine, magnesium, iron, and iodine.

- Oxygen: 65%
- Carbon: 18%
- Hydrogen: 10%
- Nitrogen: 3%
- Calcium: 1.5%
- Others: 2.5%

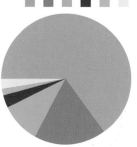

There are an estimated 30 trillion human cells in your body, but 100 trillion microbial (bacteria and fungi) cells—more than three times the amount of human cells.

How much do your feet sweat?

There are about 250,000 sweat glands in your feet, producing at least 1 cup (250 ml) of sweat every day.

Feet produce about one glassful of sweat a day.

Smelly feet is the result of body odor, which occurs when sweat mixes with bacteria on the skin.

Sweat contains tiny amounts of minerals and metals, including sodium, potassium, calcium, magnesium, zinc, copper, iron, chromium, nickel, and lead.

FAST FACTS

People's bodies produce different amounts of sweat depending on how hard they work and how hot it is.

Average: 1 quart (1 liter) per day

Moderate exercise: 6 quarts (6 liters) per day

Lots of exercise: 15 quarts (15 liters) per day

Sweat is produced in glands in the skin. A tube carries the sweat to the surface, where it is released through a pore.

Hair

Pore

Sweat gland

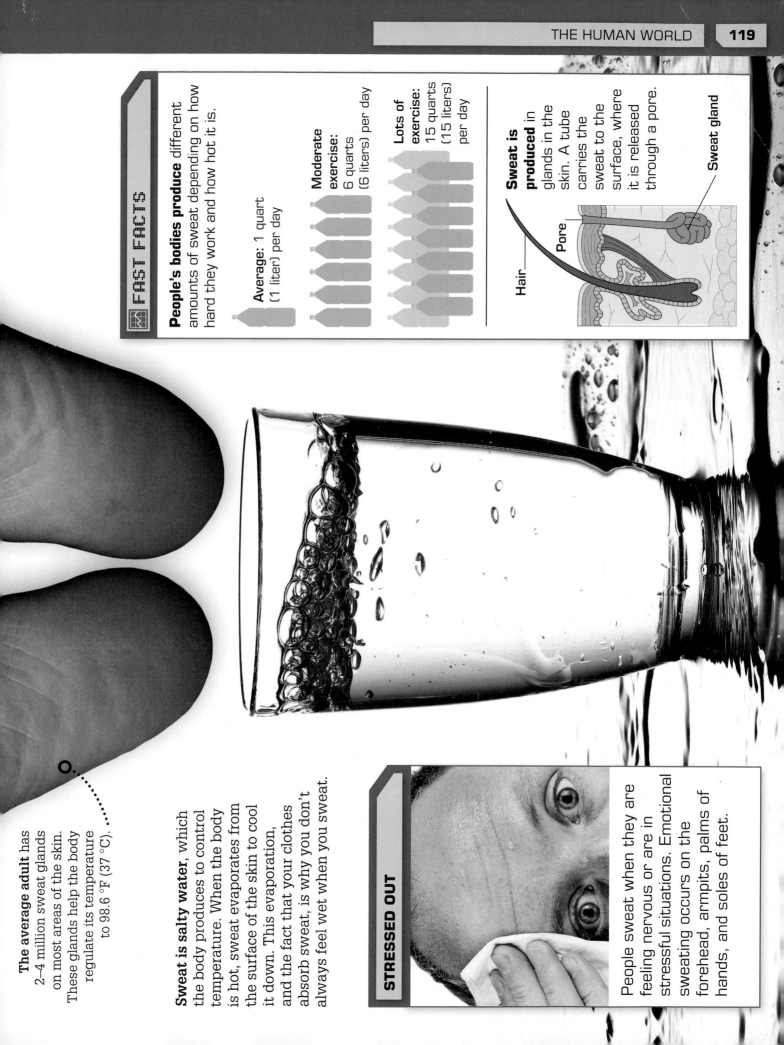

The average adult has 2–4 million sweat glands on most areas of the skin. These glands help the body regulate its temperature to 98.6 °F (37 °C).

Sweat is salty water, which the body produces to control temperature. When the body is hot, sweat evaporates from the surface of the skin to cool it down. This evaporation, and the fact that your clothes absorb sweat, is why you don't always feel wet when you sweat.

STRESSED OUT

People sweat when they are feeling nervous or are in stressful situations. Emotional sweating occurs on the forehead, armpits, palms of hands, and soles of feet.

How tiny is a virus?

Rhinoviruses are the **tiny** chemical packages that cause the common **cold**. They measure **30 nanometers** (nm) across, which is **30 billionths** of **3 ft** (1 m).

pinhead magnified **190 times**

The pin and viruses are shown here at 190 times magnification.

SPEEDY SNEEZE

A single sneeze produces more than 40,000 droplets of moisture that may contain millions of viruses and bacteria. These exit the nose at up to 80 mph (130 kph) and can travel up to 33 ft (10 m).

Around **2,267,250,000 rhinoviruses** can fit on the **head** of a **pin.**

A pinhead measures 0.06 in (1.5 mm) in diameter.

The virus's bumpy outer case, called a capsid, is seen at 900,000 times magnification.

Microscopic rhinoviruses, shown here magnified 130,000 times, are easily inhaled. The virus irritates the lining of the nose and makes it release mucus.

There are 99 known types of human rhinovirus, which are among the smallest of all human viruses. They cause almost 80 percent of colds, with symptoms including a sore throat, runny nose, headache, and sneezing.

FAST FACTS

Bacteria or virus?

A bacterium is a single-celled organism that can live anywhere. Bacteria are usually many times bigger than viruses.

Bacterium
1,000 nm long

Cell wall
(outer cover)

Flagellum
(helps cell
to move)

Chromosome
(contains genes)

Cytoplasm
(jellylike material inside cell)

A virus consists of strands of genetic material inside a capsid (case) made of protein. Viruses must invade cells to reproduce.

Virus
20–400 nm across

Capsid

Genetic
material

Surface
protein

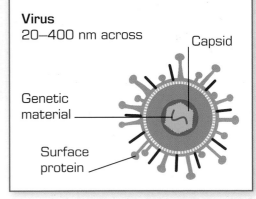

Body data

SKIN STATISTICS

Your skin is the **largest**, heaviest organ of your body. The average adult has **22 sq ft (2 m²)** of skin, which is enough to cover a doorway. • An adult's skin **can weigh more than 20 lb** (9 kg)—the same as four house bricks. • The cells that make up your skin die and fall off. We lose **30,000—40,000** dead skin cells every hour. This adds up to **105 lb** (47 kg) over a lifetime. • Your skin's upper layer is replaced **every 4 weeks.**

IN ONE YEAR, THE AVERAGE PERSON...

- grows **6 in** (15 cm) of **H A I R**.
- creates **26 gallons** (100 liters) of **tears**.
- sweats **71 gallons** (270 liters) of **SWEAT**.
- produces **159 gallons** (600 liters) of URINE and **360 lb** (160 kg) of **poop**.

DNA

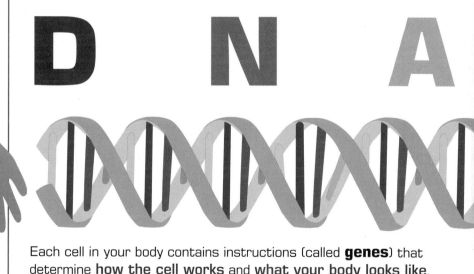

Each cell in your body contains instructions (called **genes**) that determine **how the cell works** and **what your body looks like**. The genes are carried on structures called **chromosomes**, which are made from **deoxyribonucleic acid**, or DNA.

Humans share **98 percent** of our DNA with chimps. We also share **50 percent** with bananas!

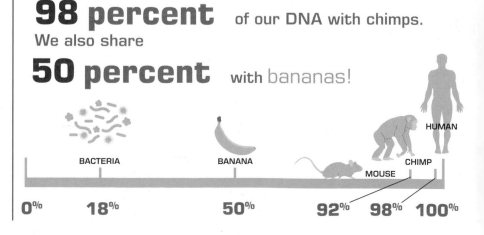

BACTERIA   BANANA   MOUSE   CHIMP   HUMAN

0%   18%   50%   92%   98%   100%

FEELING FINE

▶ Your sense of touch is incredible, with your fingers able to feel objects as small as **13 nanometers** (about one-fifth of the thickness of a hair).

WHAT NERVE!

▶ **Nerves transmit impulses** (send signals) around your body to keep it moving and working. The signals travel *to and from* the **brain** along the spinal cord.

▶ The average speed of **nerve impulses** traveling to and from the brain is

165–200 ft (50–60 meters) per second, which works out to

112–134 mph
(180–216 kph).

Stretched out

the DNA from **one cell nucleus** would be about 6 ft (1.8 m) long, which is the height of an average man.

All the DNA found in your body's cells would create a chain more than

10 billion miles (16 billion km) long.

It could reach to Pluto and back when Earth and Pluto are at their farthest apart!

HAIR RAISING

On average...

blonds have **130,000** hairs on their head.

brunettes have **110,000** hairs on their head.

redheads have **90,000** hairs on their head.

▶ Hair is made of **keratin**, the same protein found in animal hooves and claws.

Hair is made up of:
50 percent carbon,
21 percent oxygen,
17 percent nitrogen,
6 percent hydrogen,
and 5 percent sulfur.

How much **rice** is **eaten** in a **year?**

As an average across the world, each person eats **150 lb** (68 kg) of **rice** a **year**. That gives a total amount of **481,210,000 tons** (436,546,368 metric tons) eaten across the world.

The amount of **rice** eaten globally is the same weight as **84 Great Pyramids**.

Almost half of the global population eat rice regularly. Farmers in Asia produce about 90 percent of the world's rice, with China and India producing more than half of the total amount grown.

Rice is the biggest staple food for much of the world, particularly in Asia, where rice consumption is highest.

Rice comes in 40,000 varieties. Most is eaten in the region in which it is grown.

FLOODED FIELDS

Rice is grown in wet paddy fields. These are affected by climate change, and damage from droughts and floods may cut rice production by 50 percent by 2050.

More than 2.3 million blocks of stone were used in the construction of the Great Pyramid in Giza, Egypt. The largest blocks weigh 70 tons (63 metric tons) each.

The Great Pyramid weighs about 5.7 tons (5.2 million metric tons).

📈 FAST FACTS

All the rice grown in a year could cover Mongolia, which has an area of 0.6 million sq miles (1.6 million km²).

The weight of all the rice grown in a year is as heavy as 142 Great Pyramids.

What's the hottest chili pepper?

The **Carolina Reaper** holds the record for the hottest chili, hitting 1,569,300 on the **Scoville scale**. This measures how hot a chili is in Scoville Heat Units (**SHU**).

 **FAST FACTS**

A chili is the fruit of a plant that protects the seeds. The placenta is the hottest part of the pepper because it contains the most capsaicin—the chemical that makes them spicy. The endocarp also has high levels of capsaicin.

Stem — Endocarp

Seed

Placenta

In 1912 American pharmacist Wilbur Scoville devised the Scoville scale to measure how many times a chili would have to be diluted in sugar water before its heat could not be felt. This was originally judged only by an individual's taste, which was highly inaccurate. Today the scale is measured scientifically, with pure capsaicin at 16 million SHU.

Tabasco peppers are hot, but they are watered down to make tabasco sauce, which has a rating of 2,500–5,000 SHU.

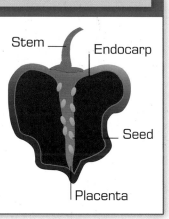

16 ×

HOTTER than jalapeño (100,000 SHU)

JALAPEÑO pepper

6 ×

HOTTER than jalapeño (30,000–50,000 SHU)

(2,500–10,000 SHU)

The Scotch bonnet chili is said to resemble a traditional Scottish tam o'shanter hat.

Although the Carolina Reaper's world record is logged at an average 1,569,300 SHU, there are claims that the hottest peaked at 2,200,000 SHU.

CHILI CONTEST

Chili-eating competitions are held in some parts of the world, with contestants experiencing watery eyes, sweaty skin, and red faces.

296 ×

HOTTER
than jalapeño
(1,500,000–
2,200,000 SHU)

140 ×

HOTTER
than jalapeño
(855,000 SHU)

The ghost pepper shows that the stronger the chili, the more wrinkly the exterior.

The official hottest Carolina Reaper was 230 times times hotter than a jalapeño pepper.

How many apples do we grow?

More than **88 million tons** (80 million metric tons) of apples are grown around the world **each year.** Because an apple weighs about **5.3 oz** (150 g), that works out to **44,900,000,000** apples every **month.**

All the apples grown in a **month** would fill **the Colosseum six times** over.

SQUARE APPLES

The packaging problems of round fruit can be solved by making them square. In Korea, some apples are grown in plastic molds so they take on a square shape.

There are thought to be 7,500 varieties of apple grown across the world. The fruit originated in central Asia thousands of years ago.

The Colosseum in Rome, Italy, was built in 80 CE for sporting events. It seated 50,000–87,000 spectators.

FAST FACTS

The 538,800,000,000 apples grown globally in a year are enough for each person on Earth to have 73.8 apples a year.

All the apples grown in a year would cover 910 sq miles (2,380 km²)—larger the entire island of Mauritius in the Indian Ocean.

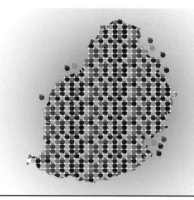

This chart shows how much fruit was grown in a year, by weight. The most popular fruit grown in the world is the banana.

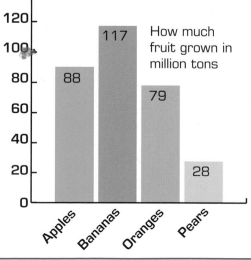

How much fruit grown in million tons

Apples 88, Bananas 117, Oranges 79, Pears 28

How much sugar is in our food?

Sugar is **added** to most of the **packaged** foods we eat and can make up **one-third** of the content. Eating too much sugar leads to **health problems**, such as tooth decay, obesity, and diabetes.

Ketchup is almost one-quarter sugar, making it a high-sugar food. It is low in fat and contains vitamins A and C, but should still be eaten sparingly.

Ketchup
16 oz (460 g)

One can of regular **soda** contains **9 teaspoonfuls** of **sugar**.

Soda
12 fl oz (330 ml)

30% SUGAR

Cereal bar
1.3 oz (35 g)

One sugar cube is 0.14 oz (4 g) of sugar, which is a teaspoonful. Just 0.03 oz (1 g) of sugar has four calories, making 16 calories in every cube.

Strawberry yogurt
4 oz (120 g)

16% SUGAR

FAST FACTS

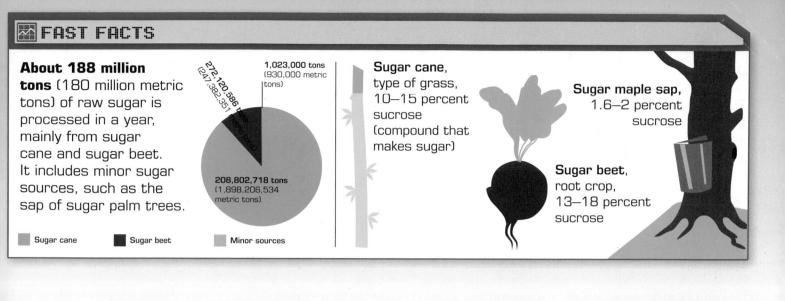

About 188 million tons (180 million metric tons) of raw sugar is processed in a year, mainly from sugar cane and sugar beet. It includes minor sugar sources, such as the sap of sugar palm trees.

272,120,586 tons (247,382,351 metric tons)

1,023,000 tons (930,000 metric tons)

208,802,718 tons (1,898,206,534 metric tons)

■ Sugar cane   ■ Sugar beet   ■ Minor sources

Sugar cane, type of grass, 10–15 percent sucrose (compound that makes sugar)

Sugar maple sap, 1.6–2 percent sucrose

Sugar beet, root crop, 13–18 percent sucrose

Orange juice
18 fl oz (500 ml)

The World Health Organization recommends the daily allowance of "free sugar" (sugar added to food) for a healthy adult is a maximum of 1.7 oz (50 g), or 12 teaspoons. This equates to no more than 10 percent of an adult's 2,000-calorie daily diet. For children, the allowance is less.

Flavored water
9 fl oz (250 ml)

Tomato soup
14 oz (400 g)

8.3% SUGAR

8% SUGAR

5% SUGAR

Which **food** has the most **vitamin C?**

Oranges are known as a source of **vitamin C,** but other **fruit** and **vegetables** contain much more. **Yellow peppers** are the **richest source** of all.

Vitamin C helps to repair bones, blood, and other body tissues. It also keeps gums healthy, helps the body absorb iron from food, protects against bruises, and heals cuts.

One orange could supply a nine-year-old plus a five-year-old with their recommended daily allowance (RDA) of vitamin C.

One yellow pepper contains almost **five times** as much **vitamin C** as an **orange**.

69.7 mg Vitamin C

PEPPERS PAST

Peppers are native to Central and South America and have been eaten since ancient times. Christopher Columbus named the pungent fruit after the hot spice pepper; he is thought to have brought them to Europe.

A single yellow pepper could supply seven nine-year-olds plus a five-year-old with their RDA of vitamin C.

341.3 mg
Vitamin C

The color of a pepper changes as it ripens, starting green, then turning yellow, and through orange to red. The level of vitamin C the pepper contains changes as it changes color, increasing from 120 mg (green) to 341.3 mg (yellow), then decreasing to 190 mg (red).

FAST FACTS

Recommended daily allowances (RDA) of vitamin C differ around the world, and recommended amounts also increase with age. This chart shows the US RDA.

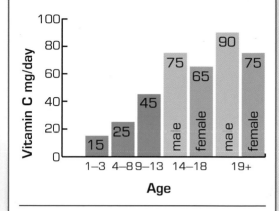

Vitamin C mg/day (y-axis, 0–100)

Age	1–3	4–8	9–13	14–18 male	14–18 female	19+ male	19+ female
mg	15	25	45	75	65	90	75

The human body cannot make or store vitamin C, so, to stay healthy, your diet must include regular amounts. Below shows how much you need to eat of certain foods to get 60 mg of vitamin C.

30 black currants

6 strawberries

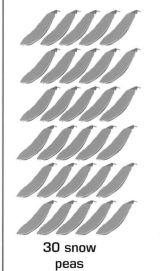

30 snow peas

85% of an orange

How much milk do we consume?

About **885 million tons** (805 million metric tons) of milk is produced each year. People don't just **drink** it: milk is used to make dairy products, including **cheese**, **butter**, and **yogurt**.

All mammals are brought up drinking milk—but humans are the only species that regularly drinks the milk of a different animal.

Each tanker has a capacity of 8,360 gallons (38,000 liters).

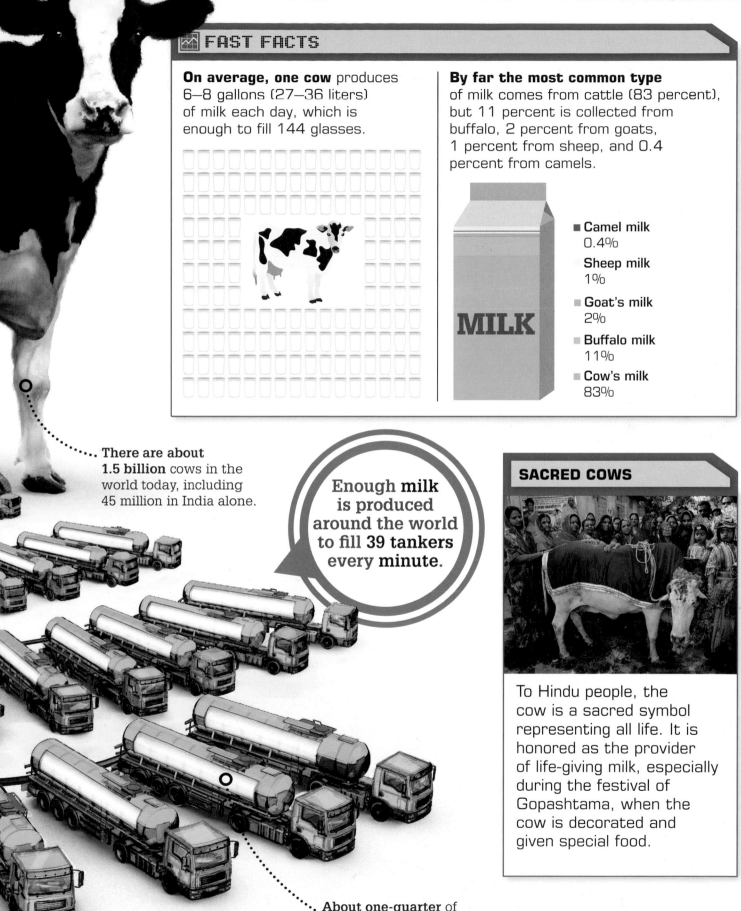

FAST FACTS

On average, one cow produces 6–8 gallons (27–36 liters) of milk each day, which is enough to fill 144 glasses.

By far the most common type of milk comes from cattle (83 percent), but 11 percent is collected from buffalo, 2 percent from goats, 1 percent from sheep, and 0.4 percent from camels.

MILK

- Camel milk 0.4%
- Sheep milk 1%
- Goat's milk 2%
- Buffalo milk 11%
- Cow's milk 83%

There are about **1.5 billion** cows in the world today, including 45 million in India alone.

Enough **milk** is produced around the world to fill **39 tankers** every **minute**.

SACRED COWS

To Hindu people, the cow is a sacred symbol representing all life. It is honored as the provider of life-giving milk, especially during the festival of Gopashtama, when the cow is decorated and given special food.

About one-quarter of all the milk collected is used in cheese production.

Food and drink data

HOW MUCH FOOD?

All the people in the world **eat** a total of **5,658 tons** (5,144 metric tons) of food **every minute**.

It would take **23 supertankers** to carry the world's food for one day. We also waste 2,719 tons (2,472 metric tons) of food **each minute**, so another **11 supertankers** would be needed to carry the world's food waste every day.

◁ Waste

Eaten food ▷

TIME FOR TEA

PRODUCTION

There are around **1,500 types** of tea.
• Tea was first brewed in China around 5,000 years ago. • More than **5½ million tons** (5 million metric tons) of tea are produced in a year—enough for a daily cup for everyone on Earth.

Tea is the world's most widely drunk beverage after water. • People in Turkey drink the most tea: **7 lb** (3.16 kg) per person each year, which works out to more than **three cups** every day. • Blocks of tea were used as currency in Siberia until **200** years ago.

CONSUMPTION

of the **eggs** laid in the world are laid in **China**—that's around **495.75 billion per year.**

%

7

3

Some **4 billion eggs** are laid every day. These could make an omelet **24.3 sq miles (63 km²)** in area, which is around **100 times** the size of **Walt Disney World, Florida**.

CHOCOLATE TREATS

- Around **4½ million tons** (4 million metric tons) of cocoa beans are produced every year • That's **12,056 tons** (10,960 metric tons) a day.
- It takes **400 cocoa beans** to make **1 lb** of chocolate (880 for 1 kg) • Two-thirds of the world's cocoa beans are grown in **Africa**, with the **Ivory Coast**, the world's leading producer, harvesting **2 million tons** (1.8 million metric tons) a year. • Europe doesn't grow any cocoa, but eight of the top ten chocolate-consuming countries are European. • Swiss people eat the most chocolate: **20 lb** (9 kg), or **180 bars** per person per year.

MORE THAN YOUR FIVE A DAY

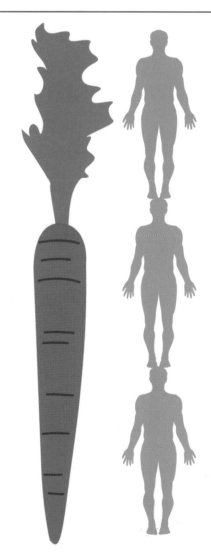

The longest carrot ever grown was **19¼ lb** (5.84 m)—three times the height of a man.

The heaviest cabbage grown weighed **138¼ lb** (62.7 kg)—the same as two children.

The heaviest lemon grown weighed **11 lb 10 oz** (5.26 kg)—about the weight of a small dog.

The largest pumpkin grown weighed **1,725 lb** (782.45 kg)—as much as a large black bear.

The heaviest tomato grown weighed **8 lb 6½ oz** (3.81 kg)—as much as a house cat.

Feats of engineering

The only limit to new design and technology is imagination. People continue to push the boundaries of engineering, dreaming up cutting-edge creations that revolutionize daily life, and our world is continually transformed as new ideas become a mass-produced reality.

The Autostadt (German for "car city") is Volkswagen's car-collection center in Germany. Up to 400 new cars can be housed inside each of the two 158-ft- (48-m-) tall glass towers. Cars are loaded into and picked from a space in the stack by an automated elevator.

How big was the *Titanic*?

At almost **883 ft** (270 m) **long**, the ill-fated *Titanic* was the **largest liner** of its day, yet it would be dwarfed by **modern cruise ships,** such as *Harmony of the Seas.*

It took two years to build the *Titanic,* which was claimed to be the safest ship ever and carried just 20 lifeboats for the 2,200 people on board. In April 1912, on its maiden voyage from the UK to New York, the *Titanic* collided with an iceberg and sank. More than 1,500 people died.

FOUR FUNNELS

The *Titanic* was built in Belfast, Northern Ireland, and is shown above on its way from the shipyard to Southampton, England. The ship had four funnels, but only three worked. The fourth was added because the builder thought it looked better.

Harmony of the Seas is **nearly five times** greater in **volume** than the *Titanic.*

HARMO

FAST FACTS

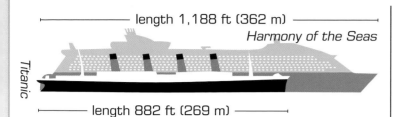

length 1,188 ft (362 m)
Harmony of the Seas

Titanic

length 882 ft (269 m)

Modern cruiseliner *Harmony of the Seas* is almost 328 ft (100 m) longer than the *Titanic*, while its beam (width) is 217 ft (66 m) compared to the *Titanic's* 92 ft (28 m).

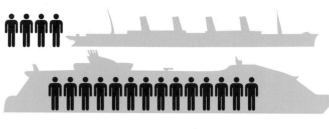

Harmony of the Seas can carry 3½ times more people than the *Titanic* did. The *Titanic* had 2,200 passengers and crew; *Harmony of the Seas* has 5,479 passengers and 2,100 crew.

The biggest cruise ship on the ocean, *Harmony of the Seas* has 16 decks and more than 2,700 rooms on board.

The doomed luxury liner *Titanic* had 10 decks and 840 rooms. There were also 20 lifeboats, used by the 705 survivors.

What's the world's biggest truck?

The **BelAZ 75710** is a huge **dump truck**, used for mining. It measures **67 ft** (20.6 m) **long**, **26 ft** (8 m) **high**, and **32 ft** (10 m) **wide**.

The BelAZ can travel at 40 mph (64 kph)—as fast as a zebra can run, but slower than a standard-size LGV (large goods vehicle). Powering the monster-size truck takes 553 gallons of diesel fuel per 100 miles (1,300 liters per 100 km).

FAST FACTS

The BelAZ 75710 could just about squeeze inside a tennis court.

249 ft (76 m)

13 miles (21 km)

If the BelAZ and a car were both given 1 gallon (4 liters) of fuel, the car would be able to travel 281 times farther than the truck.

African elephants are the largest land animals, weighing up to 5½ tons (5 metric tons).

The truck weighs 400 tons (360 metric tons), but it can carry more than it weighs, taking on 500 tons (450 metric tons).

The BelAZ 75710 could carry 90 fully grown African elephants.

Eight wheels are arranged in pairs to support the weighty truck.

75710

960

Relative size of a human and an African elephant compared to the truck

WEENY WHEELS

The Peel P50 is the world's smallest car. The three-wheeled microcar is 53 in (134 cm) long, 39 in (99 cm) wide, and 39½ in (100 cm) tall. It was manufactured on the Isle of Man, UK, in the 1960s.

How many cars are in the world?

Globally there are an estimated **1.2 billion cars**, which works out to about **one car** for every **six people**. Parked together, they would fill an area of **9,637 sq miles** (24,960 km²).

Sicily, the island off the "toe" of Italy, has a total area of 9,908 sq miles (25,662 km²).

COSTLY CAR

Cars can be a luxury item, selling for huge sums of money. In 2013, this 1963 Ferrari 250 GTO racer became the world's most expensive car when it was sold to a private buyer for $52 million.

All the **cars** in the **world** would fill an area the **size** of Sicily.

Sicily

Each car is allocated 25 sq yd (20.8 m²) to park in.

The number of "passenger cars" (cars, pickup trucks, and minibuses) in the world exceeded one billion for the first time in 2010. Today's 1.2 billion cars would fit in a parking lot almost the same size as the whole of Sicily.

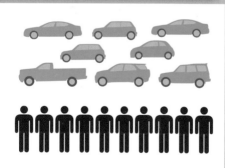

📈 FAST FACTS

Monaco has the highest rate of car ownership in the world. For every 1,000 people (including children), there are 771 passenger cars. That's almost eight vehicles for every 10 people.

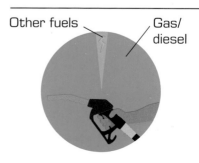

Other fuels

Gas/diesel

A whopping 97.5 percent of the world's cars are powered by gas or diesel. The remaining 2.5 percent are electric, plug-in hybrid, or fuel-cell vehicles.

The world's best-selling car is the Toyota Corolla, with 40 million cars sold in at least 150 countries.

How **big** is the **biggest plane?**

The **largest** and **heaviest** airplane to take flight is the Russian cargo jet **Antonov An-225**. Built to carry the Soviet space shuttle *Buran*, its maximum takeoff weight is **1.32 million lb** (600,000 kg) and it is **275 ft** (84 m) long.

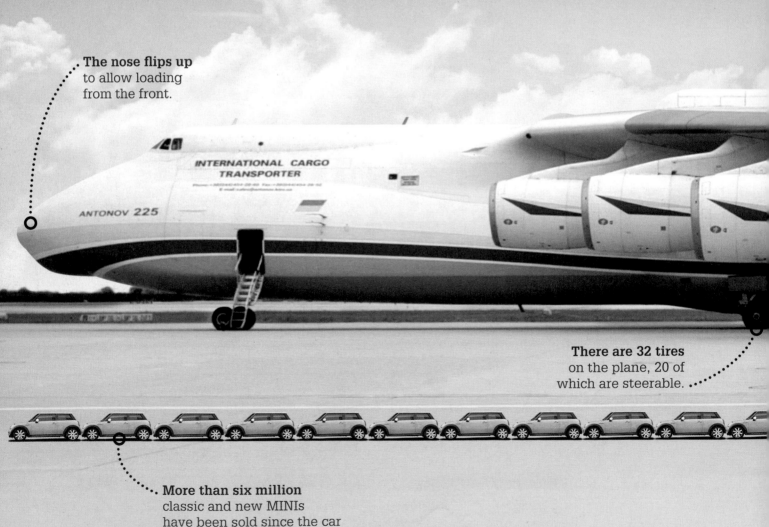

The nose flips up to allow loading from the front.

There are 32 tires on the plane, 20 of which are steerable.

More than six million classic and new MINIs have been sold since the car was first produced in 1959.

FAST FACTS

The An-225 is the longest plane, but another has a bigger wingspan—the Hughes H-4 Spruce Goose, a World War II military prototype.

An-225 290 ft (88.4 m)

Hughes H-4 320 ft (97.5 m)

Tailfin 59½ ft (18.1 m)

To be level with the tailfin of the An-225, a person must look from a fifth-story window.

PIGGYBACK PLANE

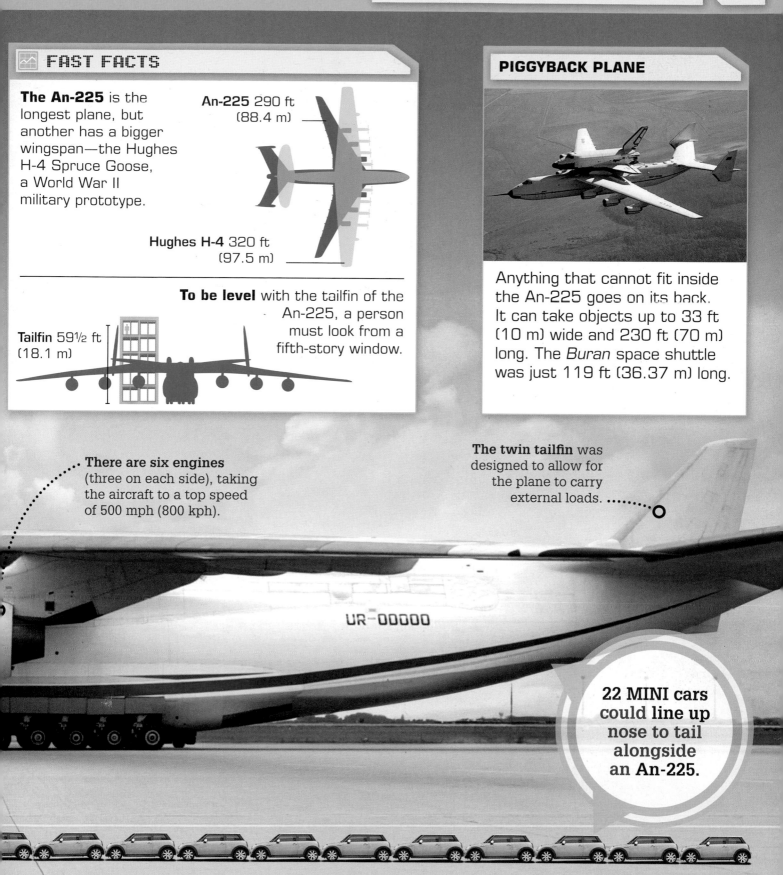

Anything that cannot fit inside the An-225 goes on its back. It can take objects up to 33 ft (10 m) wide and 230 ft (70 m) long. The *Buran* space shuttle was just 119 ft (36.37 m) long.

There are six engines (three on each side), taking the aircraft to a top speed of 500 mph (800 kph).

The twin tailfin was designed to allow for the plane to carry external loads.

UR-00000

22 MINI cars could line up nose to tail alongside an An-225.

There is only one An-225—a second was partly built and remains in storage. The aircraft is nicknamed Myria, which is Russian for "dream." At the time of the An-225's first flight in 1988, it was 50 percent larger than any other aircraft.

How **big** is the **biggest** submarine?

Russia's **Typhoon-Class** is the largest submarine ever built. It measures **574 ft** (175 m) long, **70 ft** (23 m) wide, and weighs **29,000 tons** (26,500 metric tons). The Typhoon is designed for **size**, **speed**, and **deep dives**.

Only six Typhoon-Class submarines were built, and just one remains in operation today. These nuclear-powered ballistic missile submarines were developed in the 1970s for the Russian Navy, but were phased out at the end of the Soviet Union's Cold War with the West.

Two large nuclear reactors inside the Typhoon submarine provide the power.

In Russia, Typhoon-Class is called Project 941 Akula Class, and is nicknamed "Shark."

The Typhoon-Class is the same length as 350 children stood shoulder-to-shoulder.

📊 FAST FACTS

A Typhoon-Class submarine can reach a maximum depth of 1,300 ft (400 m). This is deeper than the height of the Eiffel Tower in Paris, France.

Each Typhoon submarine carried a crew of 150 on board, which would fill up three buses.

Typhoon is almost half the length of the *TI Oceania*—one of the longest supertankers in the sea today.

TI Oceania
1,246 ft (380 m)

Typhoon
574 ft (175 m)

Typhoon can stay submerged for at least 120 days. The only restriction is the crew must bring in new food supplies after that time.

The maximum speed underwater is 30 mph (50 kph), which is the same as a blue whale over a short distance.

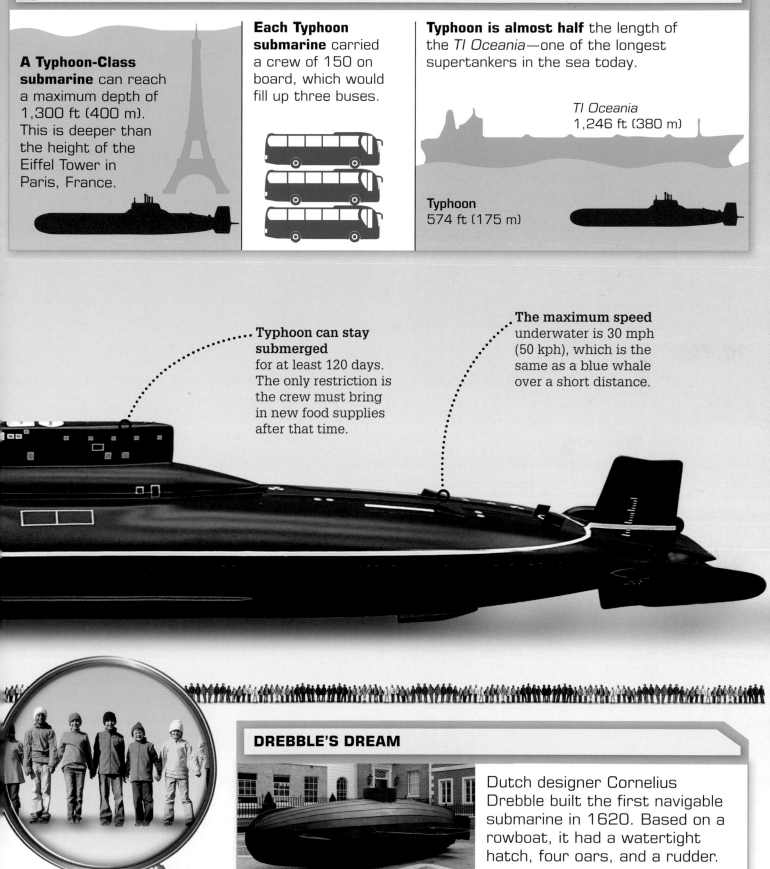

DREBBLE'S DREAM

Dutch designer Cornelius Drebble built the first navigable submarine in 1620. Based on a rowboat, it had a watertight hatch, four oars, and a rudder.

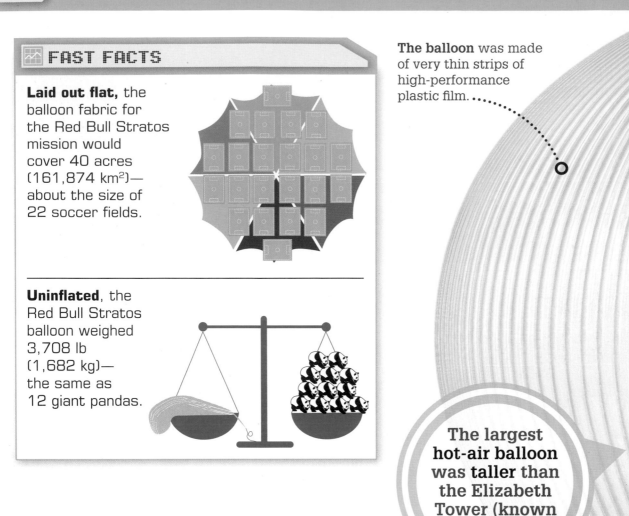

FAST FACTS

Laid out flat, the balloon fabric for the Red Bull Stratos mission would cover 40 acres (161,874 km²)— about the size of 22 soccer fields.

Uninflated, the Red Bull Stratos balloon weighed 3,708 lb (1,682 kg)— the same as 12 giant pandas.

The balloon was made of very thin strips of high-performance plastic film.

The largest hot-air balloon was **taller** than the Elizabeth Tower (known as **Big Ben**).

How **big** is the **largest** hot-air balloon?

The Red Bull Stratos hot-air balloon was **334 ft** (102 m) **tall**. It carried Austrian skydiver Felix Baumgartner **24 miles** (39 km) into the atmosphere so he could freefall and **parachute** back to Earth.

At launch, the Red Bull Stratos balloon was as tall as a 55-story building. As the balloon climbed higher in the sky, the helium gas expanded to fill the balloon slowly, giving it an almost perfectly round shape.

Hot-air balloons are the oldest form of human flight, comprising a balloon (called an envelope), burners, and a basket.

Houses of Parliament, London, UK

The balloon fabric was so delicate that it could never be used again.

Average-size hot-air balloon

What's the longest subway in the world?

Adding together all 18 lines of the subway in **Seoul**, South Korea, gives a distance of **614 miles** (987.5 km)—long enough to cross several countries!

This map shows how far you could travel on the five longest underground systems if they all started in Paris, France. All routes are direct, as the crow flies, and crossing water if necessary.

ENGLAND

Beijing Subway
327 miles (527 km)

China's capital city subway could reach from Paris to central England.

London Underground
250 miles (402 km)

Paris, FRANCE

The world's oldest underground system, found in the UK, could run from Paris to La Rochelle on France's coast.

FAST FACTS

Underground networks can have hundreds of stations. The runaway winner is the New York City Subway, with more than 100 more stations than its closest challenger.

NYC Subway—468

Shanghai Metro—337

Beijing Subway—319

Seoul Subway—311
(lines 1–9 only)

Paris Metro—303

At 33.5 miles (53.85 km) long, Japan's Seikan Tunnel is the world's longest undersea rail tunnel, with 40 percent 330 ft (100 m) below the seabed.

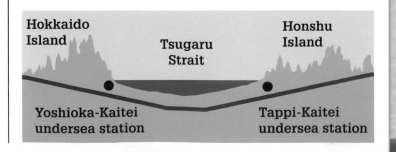

Hokkaido Island

Tsugaru Strait

Honshu Island

Yoshioka-Kaitei undersea station

Tappi-Kaitei undersea station

New York Subway
232 miles (373 km)

Seoul Metropolitan Subway
614 miles (987.5 km)

Shanghai Metro
340 miles (548 km)

The world's longest subway (including all 18 lines, some of which travel beyond Seoul) could just reach inside Poland.

America's busiest subway could take you to Rotterdam in the Netherlands.

Seoul's subway could stretch from **Paris** to **Poland**.

The subway system for China's biggest city could break into northern Italy.

NETHERLANDS
POLAND
BELGIUM
LUXEMBOURG
GERMANY
CZECH REPUBLIC
SWITZERLAND
AUSTRIA
ITALY

TIGHT SQUEEZE

Japan's capital is home to the world's busiest underground. The Tokyo Subway carries more than 3 billion people a year, with white-gloved train-pushers squeezing them onto already packed carriages.

How many shipwrecks are there?

SHALLOW WATERS

Shipwrecks are not confined to the open seas. Sunk in 1885, *Sweepstakes* lies just 20 ft (6 m) underwater in Big Tub Harbor, on the edge of Lake Huron in Canada.

There are more than **160,000 shipwrecks** whose positions have been mapped in the world's oceans.

It is likely the total number of wrecks, from warships to liners, runs into millions. By comparison, there are about 50,420 merchant ships (ships that transport cargo or passengers) currently sailing the oceans.

Viking ship

Phoenician bireme

HMS Sussex (1694)

FAST FACTS

The deepest shipwreck found is a German World War II vessel in the South Atlantic Ocean. At 18,904 ft (5,762 m) down, it lies almost as deep as Mount Kilimanjaro is tall.

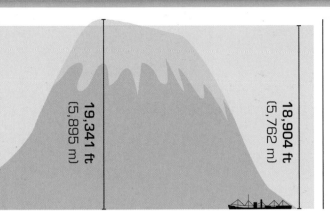

19,341 ft (5,895 m)

18,904 ft (5,762 m)

Shipwrecks contain an estimated $60 billion of treasure, which works out as $8 for every person in the world.

Container ships, known as "box boats," transport at least 200 million containers a year.

There are more shipwrecks under the sea than there are ships at sea.

RMS Lusitania
(1915)

Bismark
(1941)

USS Arizona
(1942)

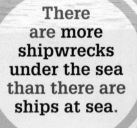

HMS Birkenhead
(1852)

Buildings data

YOU SPIN ME RIGHT ROUND

The world's **first residential block** to have independently rotating floors was completed in 2001 and is located in **Curitiba, Paraná, Brazil**. It has 11 floors that can each rotate clockwise or counterclockwise, and it takes 1 hour for these to rotate the full **360 degrees**.

SKYSCRAPER CITIES

HONG KONG
314 SKYSCRAPERS

NEW YORK CITY
240 SKYSCRAPERS

DUBAI
152 SKYSCRAPERS

A skyscraper is a building taller than *492 ft* (150 m). The taller the tower, the more that can be packed into a city.

TALLEST STRUCTURES

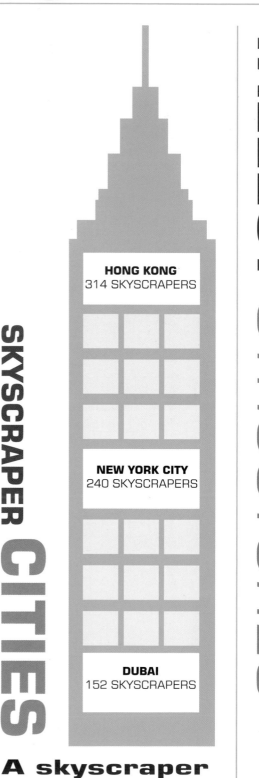

2,625 FT (800 M)
2,300 FT (700 M)
1,970 FT (600 M)
1,640 FT (500 M)
1,310 FT (400 M)
985 FT (300 M)
655 FT (200 M)
330 FT (100 M)

TALLEST BUILDING: *BURJ KHALIFA, DUBAI* 2,716 FT (828 M)

The Burj Khalifa in Dubai is the world's tallest building, but there are many other tall structures around the world that hold their own titles.

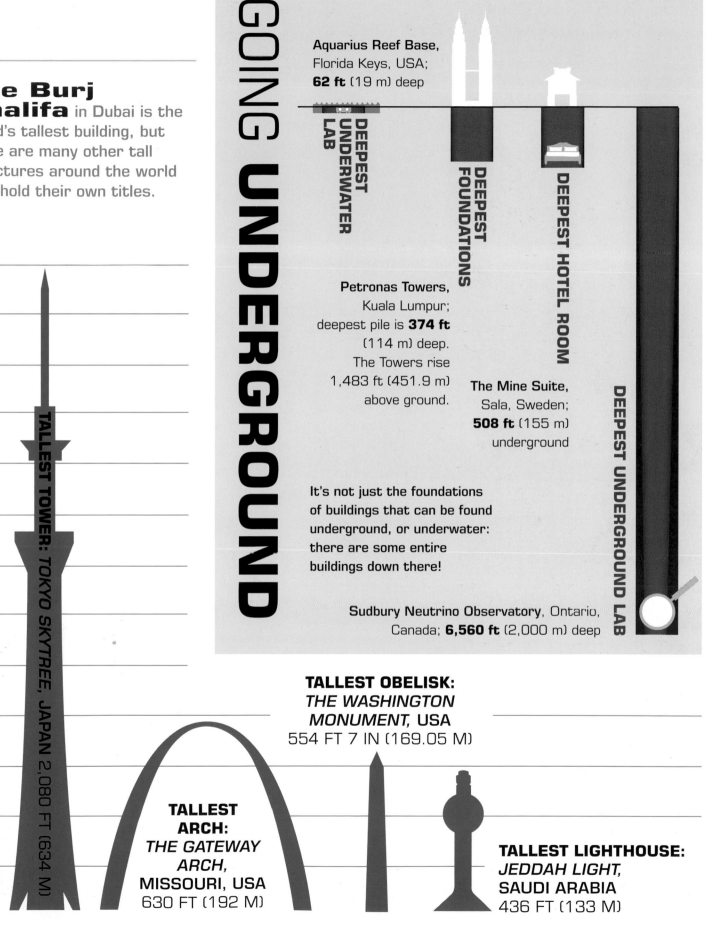

GOING UNDERGROUND

Aquarius Reef Base, Florida Keys, USA; **62 ft** (19 m) deep

DEEPEST UNDERWATER LAB

DEEPEST FOUNDATIONS

Petronas Towers, Kuala Lumpur; deepest pile is **374 ft** (114 m) deep. The Towers rise 1,483 ft (451.9 m) above ground.

DEEPEST HOTEL ROOM

The Mine Suite, Sala, Sweden; **508 ft** (155 m) underground

DEEPEST UNDERGROUND LAB

It's not just the foundations of buildings that can be found underground, or underwater: there are some entire buildings down there!

Sudbury Neutrino Observatory, Ontario, Canada; **6,560 ft** (2,000 m) deep

TALLEST TOWER: *TOKYO SKYTREE, JAPAN* 2,080 FT (634 M)

TALLEST ARCH: *THE GATEWAY ARCH,* MISSOURI, USA 630 FT (192 M)

TALLEST OBELISK: *THE WASHINGTON MONUMENT,* USA 554 FT 7 IN (169.05 M)

TALLEST LIGHTHOUSE: *JEDDAH LIGHT,* SAUDI ARABIA 436 FT (133 M)

158

FAST FACTS

India's Statue of Unity will be the world's tallest statue when completed. At 597 ft (182 m), it will be three times the height of Italy's Leaning Tower of Pisa.

The largest of the Easter Island Moai statues stands 33 ft (10 m) high, while the heaviest weighs 95 tons (86 metric tons)—the same as seven school buses.

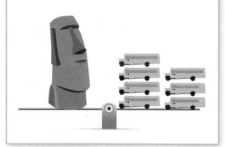

This statue depicting the Vairocana Buddha is made from 238 lb (108 kg) of gold, 3,600 tons (3,300 metric tons) of copper, and 17,500 tons (15,000 metric tons) of steel.

The world's largest statues often pay tribute to a god, leader, or other influential figure, with the size of the sculpture and the materials used emphasizing the person's significance. The heights given here include bases.

Spring Temple Buddha, Henan, China
682 ft (208 m)

Spring Temple Buddha is more than **twice as tall** as the **Statue of Liberty**.

Laykyun Setkyar Standing Buddha, Burma (Myanmar)
423¼ ft (129 m)

How **tall** is the **tallest statue**?

The **Spring Temple Buddha** or Zhongyuan Buddha is the world's **tallest** statue, with the Buddha and lotus base reaching **418¾ ft** (127.64 m) tall. With extra bases added since, the structure now stands at **682 ft** (208 m).

The Statue of Liberty was a gift from France to the US in 1886. Visitors must climb 354 stairs to reach the crown.

TERRA-COTTA ARMY

Discovered in 1974, China's terra-cotta army is a collection of more than 8,000 life-size terra-cotta statues, each with individual facial features. They are part of Emperor Qin Shi Huang's burial complex.

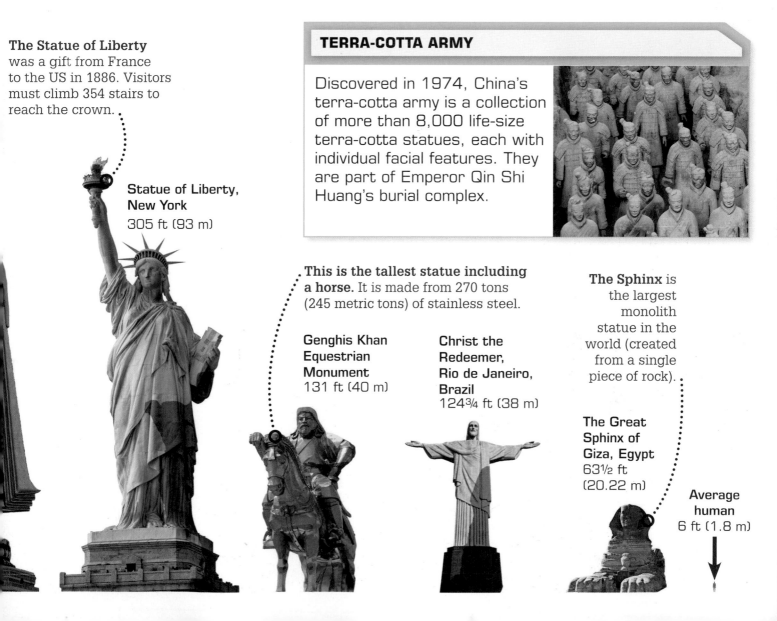

Statue of Liberty, New York
305 ft (93 m)

This is the tallest statue including a horse. It is made from 270 tons (245 metric tons) of stainless steel.

Genghis Khan Equestrian Monument
131 ft (40 m)

Christ the Redeemer, Rio de Janeiro, Brazil
124¾ ft (38 m)

The Sphinx is the largest monolith statue in the world (created from a single piece of rock).

The Great Sphinx of Giza, Egypt
63½ ft (20.22 m)

Average human
6 ft (1.8 m)

What's the fastest ball in sports?

The **official world record** goes to a **golf ball**, which was hit at a **driving range** (golf practice area) in Orlando, Florida, in January 2013.

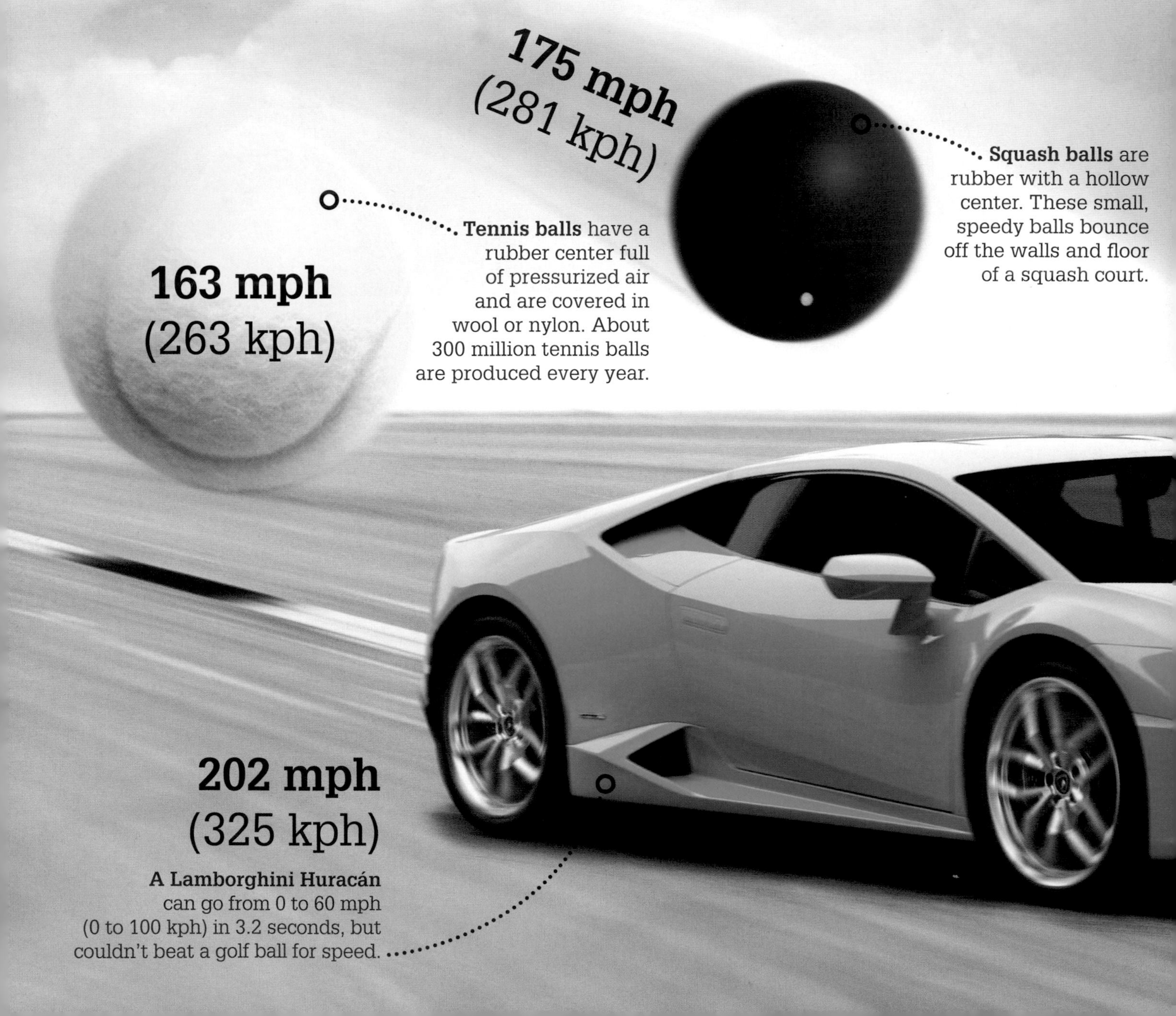

175 mph
(281 kph)

163 mph
(263 kph)

Tennis balls have a rubber center full of pressurized air and are covered in wool or nylon. About 300 million tennis balls are produced every year.

Squash balls are rubber with a hollow center. These small, speedy balls bounce off the walls and floor of a squash court.

202 mph
(325 kph)

A Lamborghini Huracán can go from 0 to 60 mph (0 to 100 kph) in 3.2 seconds, but couldn't beat a golf ball for speed.

The speed of a golf ball is measured immediately after the golf club hits the ball. The speed is the result of how fast the golf club is swung and how hard it hits the ball. The faster the ball speed, the farther the ball travels. Increasing speed by just 1 mph (1.6 kph) can add up to 2 yards (1.8 m) to the distance.

Golf balls were once basic balls crafted from wood. Today they are rubber balls covered with dimpled resin, designed to carry them higher and farther on the golf course.

217 mph (349 kph)

188 mph (302 kph)

Pelota balls have a wooden core surrounded by layers of latex (a natural rubber) and covered in goat skin. Set in 1979, the previous record for fastest ball was a pelota ball.

At **217 mph (349 kph),** the **golf ball is faster** than a **Lamborghini.**

📈 FAST FACTS

Badminton birdie
306 mph (493 kph)

Soccer ball
130 mph (210 kph)

Hockey ball
114 mph (183 kph)

Baseball
108 mph (174 kph)

Cricket
100 mph (161 kph)

Table tennis
70 mph (112 kph)

A birdie is a flying cone of feathers or plastic, and so, strictly speaking, not a ball. However, one birdie blew all the balls out of the park when a player smashed it at more than 300 mph (500 kph) in 2013.

The Golden Gate Bridge in California stretches 8,981 ft (2,737 m) across the Golden Gate strait, connecting San Francisco to Marin County.

A standard pencil is 7½ in (19 cm) long, with the average diameter measuring about ¼ in (7 mm). The traditional wooden casing was invented in the mid 16th-century: before then, graphite was wrapped in string or sheepskin.

📈 FAST FACTS

A pencil lasts 62 times longer than a pen. You would need 62 pens to draw a line the same length as one pencil can.

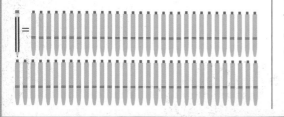

More than 14 billion pencils are used every year around the world. Laid end to end, these could circle the globe 60 times.

How **far** could a **pencil** draw?

It is estimated that a **typical pencil** has enough **graphite** to draw a line **35 miles** (56 km) long, but no one has actually tested this!

The "lead" in a pencil is actually graphite, which has been used in pencils since the early 16th century. When graphite was first discovered, it was thought to be a kind of lead.

One pencil could draw a line **20 times** the length of the **Golden Gate Bridge.**

MINIATURE JUMBOS

Russian artist Salavat Fidai carves tiny sculptures into pencil tips using a craft knife—and a magnifying glass! Each work takes between six hours and two days to make.

What's the most extreme roller coaster?

The most forceful roller coaster is "Tower of Terror" at Gold Reef City in Johannesburg, South Africa. At the bottom of the ride's huge drop, people experience a G-force of 6.3 g.

SPACE SHUTTLE 3 g

During a space shuttle launch, an astronaut experiences a maximum force of 3 g.

FIGHTER PLANE 8–9 g

Fighter pilots are trained to withstand a maximum of 9 g. They wear "g-suits" to stop blood from sinking to their legs and keep it flowing to the brain.

Tower of Terror riders experience twice the G-force of a space shuttle launch.

ROLLERCOASTER 6.3 g

The rollercoaster features a vertical drop of 154 ft (47 m) from the top of an authentic mineshaft tower.

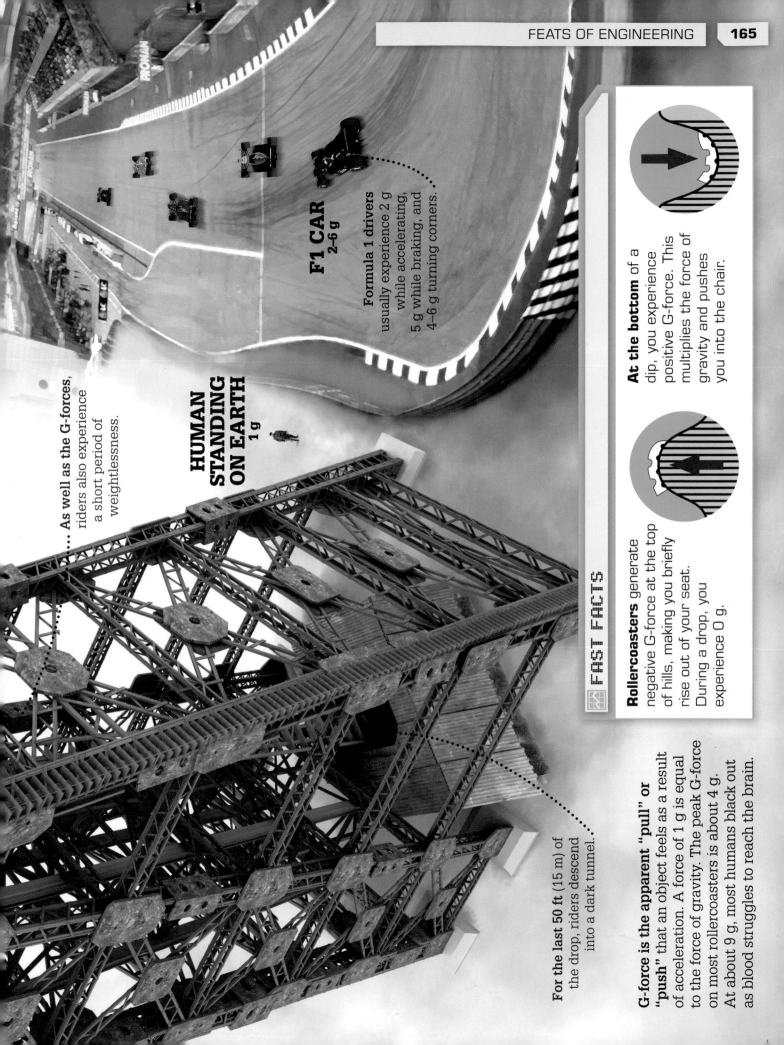

F1 CAR
2–6 g

Formula 1 drivers usually experience 2 g while accelerating, 5 g while braking, and 4–6 g turning corners.

HUMAN STANDING ON EARTH
1 g

..... As well as the G-forces, riders also experience a short period of weightlessness.

For the last 50 ft (15 m) of the drop, riders descend into a dark tunnel.

At the bottom of a dip, you experience positive G-force. This multiplies the force of gravity and pushes you into the chair.

FAST FACTS

Rollercoasters generate negative G-force at the top of hills, making you briefly rise out of your seat. During a drop, you experience 0 g.

G-force is the apparent "pull" or "push" that an object feels as a result of acceleration. A force of 1 g is equal to the force of gravity. The peak G-force on most rollercoasters is about 4 g. At about 9 g, most humans black out as blood struggles to reach the brain.

How many solar panels could power the world?

SOLAR-POWERED WINGS

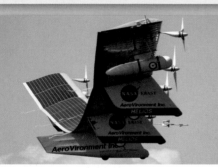

NASA's Helios Prototype was a solar powered, remote-controlled, unmanned aircraft. It holds the record for the highest non-rocket powered flight, reaching 96,863 ft (29,524 m). It crashed into the Pacific in 2003.

Spain (shown in orange) has an area of 195,364 sq miles (505,992 km^2), so the amount of solar panels needed would have to extend into Portugal (shown in green) as well.

Solar panels absorb the light from the Sun's rays and convert it into electricity or heating. Today, solar panels are not very efficient: only around 15 percent of the sunlight that hits the panel gets turned into electricity you can use. In future, as solar panels improve, fewer panels will be needed to generate the same amount of power.

If the **whole world** were powered by **solar panels**, the amount needed would cover an enormous area of **206,282 sq miles** (534,268 km^2).

> **Solar panels** to power the **world** would cover an area **bigger** than Spain.

The solar panels would provide the estimated 213,707,423,840,000 kWh (kilowatt-hours) of electricity, needed to run the world's machinery, technology, transportation, homes, and more.

FAST FACTS

Most of the world's power comes from non-renewable fossil fuels such as coal, oil, and gas. Less than one-fifth of power comes from renewable alternatives, including solar power.

- Fossil fuels 78.3%
- Traditional biomass 9%
- Nuclear power 2.6%
- Biomass/geothermal/solar heat 4.1%
- Hydropower 3.9%
- Wind 1.3%
- Biofuels 0.8%

Internet data

VIDEO VS. YOUTUBE

The first-ever commercial *video tape recorder*, which was made in 1956, was the size of a **piano!** Videos could hold around *4 hours* of material, the same amount that is now uploaded to **YouTube** every *0.6 seconds*.

WHO'S OUT THERE?

Almost **two-thirds** (61.5 percent) of internet traffic is not generated by humans, but is **unwanted** spam or junk automatically sent by **bots** and **malware**.

PERCENTAGE DIFFERENCE

The **percentage of people** who are online varies widely across different countries: from **Iceland,** with 100 percent of its population having access to the internet, to **Eritrea,** with a mere 1.1 percent online.

- Eritrea **1.1%**
- Ethiopia **4%**
- Iraq **13%**
- Angola **23%**
- Egypt **33%**
- China **52%**
- USA **88.5%**
- UK **92.6%**
- Denmark **96.3%**
- Bermuda **97.4%**
- Norway **98%**
- Iceland **100%**

GOOGLE IT

A single *Google* query uses **1,000 computers** to retrieve an answer in **0.2 seconds**.

Around 15 percent of the searches *Google* gets each day have never been *Googled* before.

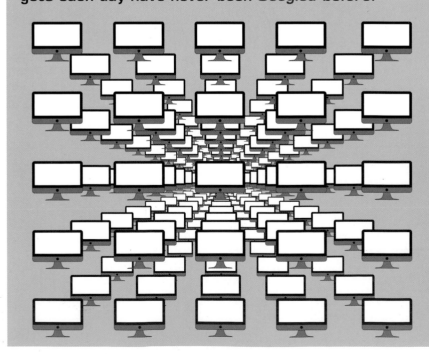

INTERNET **USERS**

Use of the internet has boomed in the last **20 years**. In December 1995, **0.4 percent** of the world's population used the Net; by December 2015, this had zoomed up to an estimated **46.4 percent**.

Number of users, in millions

Year	Users
1995	16 MILLION
2000	361 MILLION
2005	1,018 MILLION
2010	1,971 MILLION
2015	3,366 MILLION

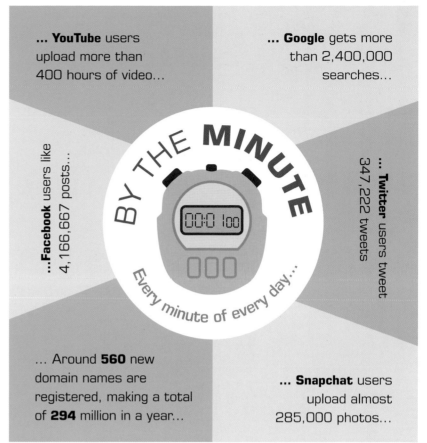

BY THE MINUTE

Every minute of every day...

... **YouTube** users upload more than 400 hours of video...

... **Google** gets more than 2,400,000 searches...

...**Facebook** users like 4,166,667 posts...

... **Twitter** users tweet 347,222 tweets

... Around **560** new domain names are registered, making a total of **294** million in a year...

... **Snapchat** users upload almost 285,000 photos...

UNDER THE *SEA*

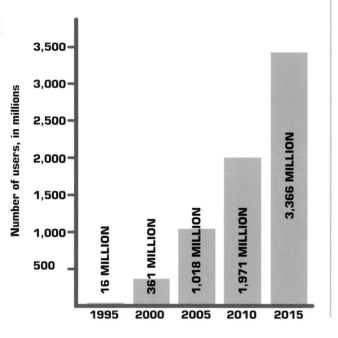

Around **99 percent** of the world's internet traffic travels via **undersea cables**. There are more than **613,009 miles** (986,543 km) of submarine communication cables— enough to reach the Moon **2.5 times**!

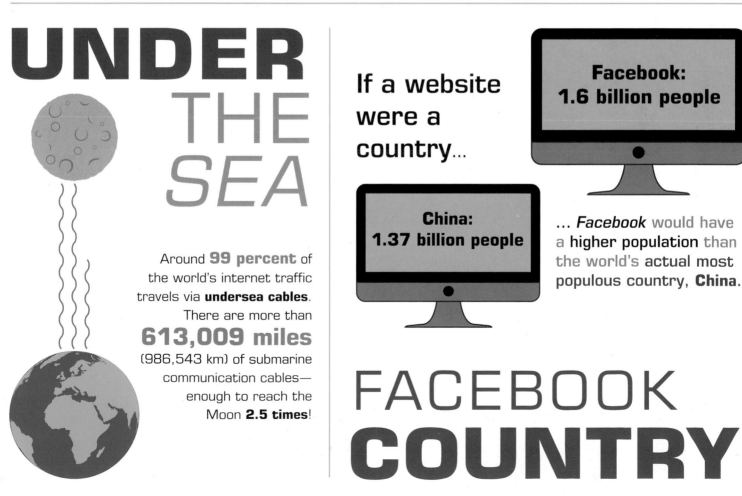

If a website were a country...

Facebook: 1.6 billion people

China: 1.37 billion people

... *Facebook* would have a higher population than the world's actual most populous country, **China**.

FACEBOOK COUNTRY

Which film cost the most to make?

The **cinematic boom** of the 21st century has made **big budget** movies with spectacular **special effects** now the norm. At **$398 million**, *Pirates of the Caribbean: On Stranger Tides* is the costliest film to date.

Three of the 10 most expensive movies are *Pirates of the Caribbean*, with costs of over $1 billion.

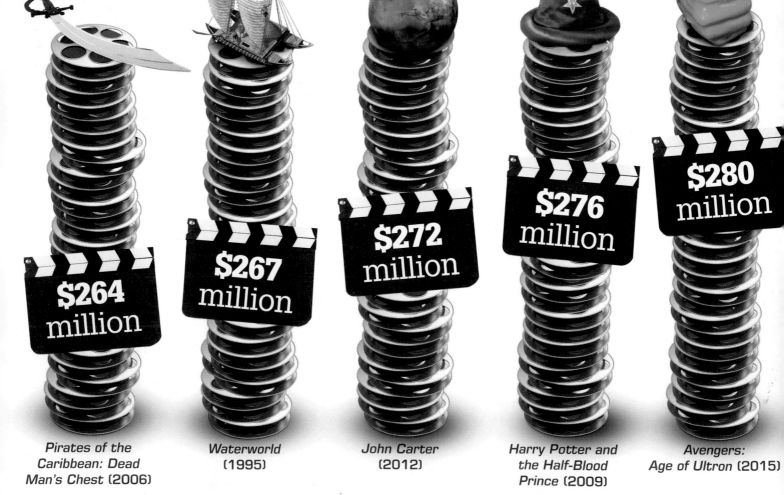

$264 million

$267 million

$272 million

$276 million

$280 million

Pirates of the Caribbean: Dead Man's Chest (2006)

Waterworld (1995)

John Carter (2012)

Harry Potter and the Half-Blood Prince (2009)

Avengers: Age of Ultron (2015)

FAST FACTS

The most expensive "back-to-back" production (set of movies) was *The Hobbit* trilogy (2012–14), which cost $745 million. This is larger than some countries' GDP (gross domestic product; how much all their goods and services are worth in a year).

Amount in millions of dollars

800
700
600
500
400
300
200
100
0

Dominica   *The Hobbit* trilogy   Comoros   Gambia

Some movie stars are paid huge sums of money. The highest-paid actor in 2015 earned almost one-third more than the highest-paid actress—a difference of $30 million.

Robert Downey Jr.
$80 million

Jennifer Lawrence
$52 million

These are the top 10 most costly films ever made, and eight of them were made in the 21st century. The amounts have been adjusted in line with inflation so all the movies can be judged on equal value.

$282 million

$294 million

$295 million

$342 million

$398 million

Tangled
(2010)

Spider-Man 3
(2007)

Titanic
(1997)

Pirates of the Caribbean: At World's End (2007)

Pirates of the Caribbean: On Stranger Tides (2011)

How big is the biggest screen?

The world's **largest permanent projection screen** can be seen at **Hengqin Ocean Kingdom** theme park in **China**.

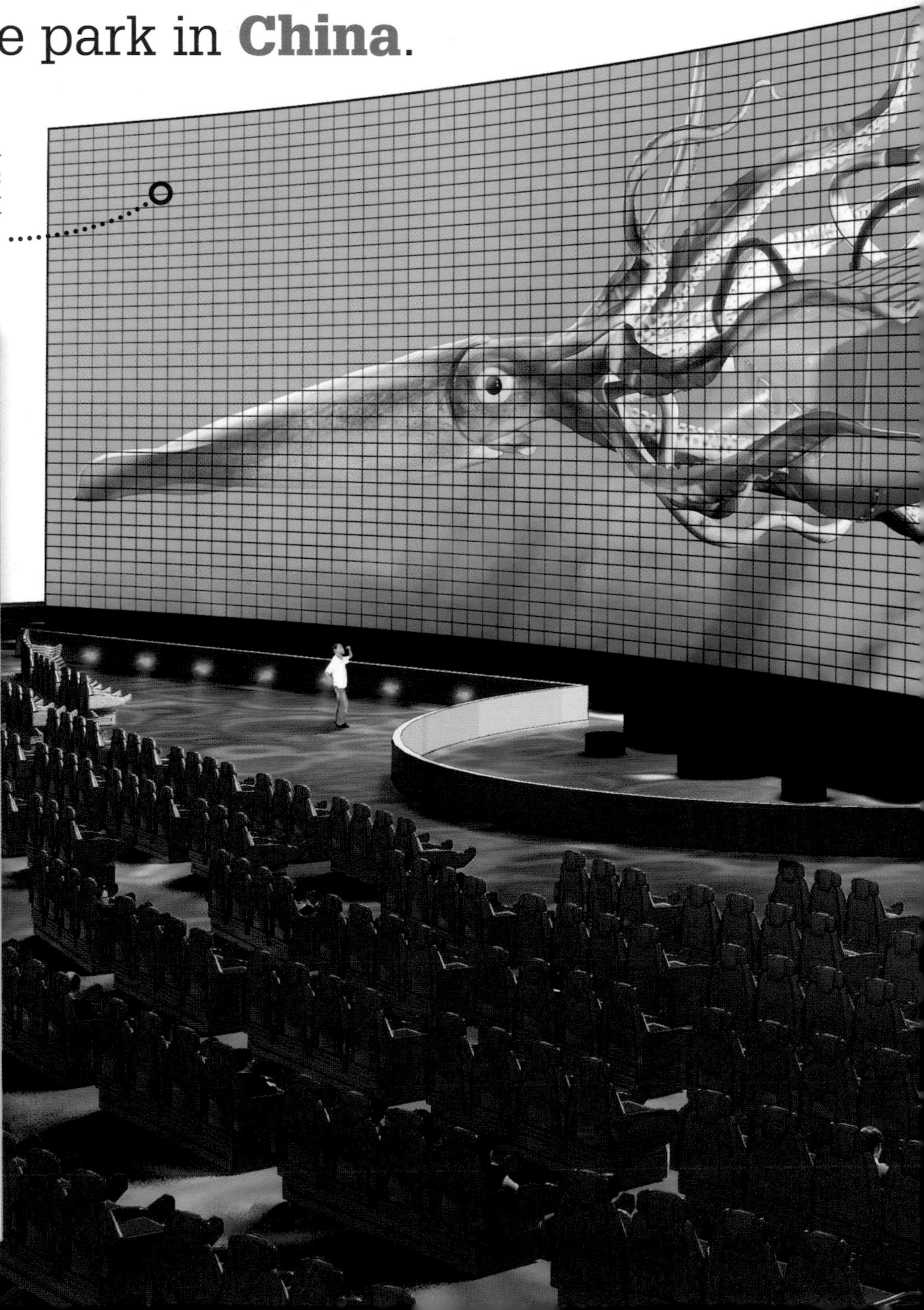

With an area of more than 17,000 sq ft (1,580 m^2), the screen sits in a theater as big as five IMAX theaters and has 1,000 hi-tech seats.

FAST FACTS

The largest true TV screen is "Big Hoss" at the Texas Motor Speedway in Fort Worth. At 218 x 94½ ft (66.4 x 22.8 m), it is longer than a Boeing 767 and taller than a 7-story building.

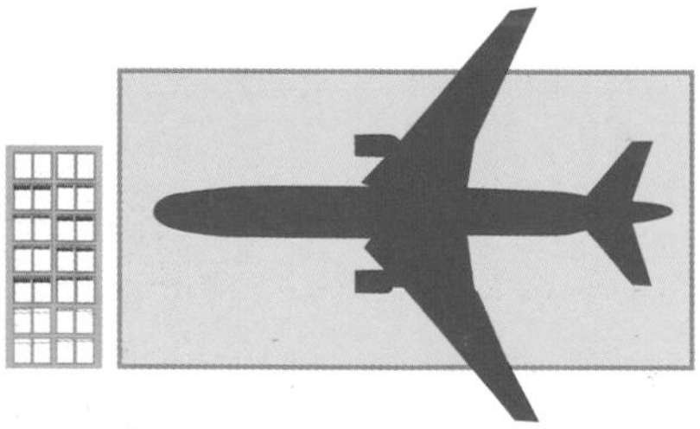

The "Viva Vision" LED display board in Las Vegas has 12.5 million LED lamps and is 1,500 ft (457 m) long—as long as 4½ soccer fields.

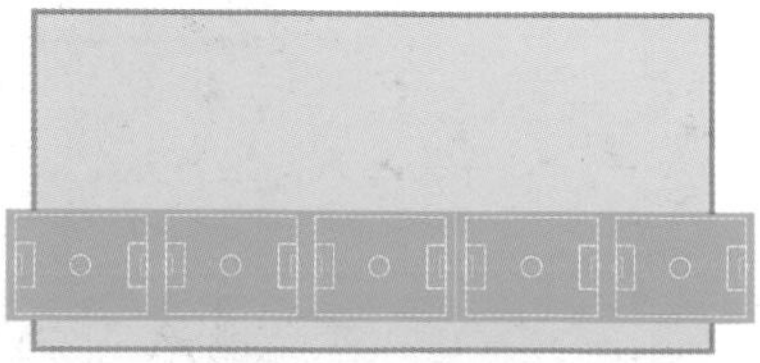

Hengqin Ocean Kingdom's projection screen is 288 ft (88 m) wide and 59 ft (18 m) high. Although it screens giant visuals, it is not a television screen, so cannot receive broadcasts. This theme park in Zhuhai set other world records at its opening in 2014, including the largest aquarium and the biggest underwater viewing dome.

Here, a grid has been placed over the screen to show it is the same size as 4,000 televisions 32 in (82 cm) wide and 18 in (46 cm) tall.

The **Hengqin Ocean Kingdom screen** is about the size of **4,000** average-size televisions.

How small is the smallest camera?

The **smallest** camera in the world is smaller than a **grain of sand**, at just **0.039 in** (1 mm) wide. The **microcamera** is used to see inside people's bodies during operations.

The medical microcamera has a resolution of 45,000 pixels, which is about one-twentieth of a megapixel.

> The smallest camera is 375 times smaller than a mobile phone's **SIM** card.

📈 FAST FACTS

The first photograph was taken in 1814. Today, the number of photographs taken every two minutes is the same as the number of pictures taken by the whole world in the 1800s.

1800s:
A few million

1960s:
3 billion a year

2000:
86 billion

2012:
More than 380 billion

The SIM circuit of a standard mobile phone contains the phone user's details and contacts. "SIM" stands for "Subscriber Identity Module."

PICTURE OF HEALTH

Endoscopes are often inserted into the body via the mouth. Images of the area being examined, such as the throat, are sent back for the doctor or surgeon to view on screen during the procedure.

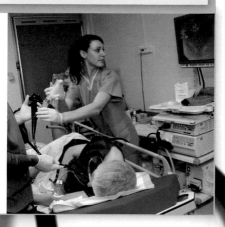

The microcamera is housed at the end of an endoscope, which is a long, flexible tube used to look inside the body. There is also a light at the end.

A mini SIM card measures 1 x 0.6 in (25 mm x 15 mm). The plastic "smart card" has a microprocessor to connect your phone to the service provider and to store data.

SIM card and camera shown actual size

CHINESE SUPERPOWER

Today's most powerful computer is China's Tianhe 2 ("Milky Way 2"), with a 1,375-tebibyte (1.4 million gigabyte) memory. It can perform 100,000 times as many tasks as there are stars in the Milky Way every second.

Weighty ENIAC featured 40 panels and filled a room with its vast size. To perform each new task, its plugs and switches had to be moved (reprogrammed) by hand.

20 YEARS

At the time, ENIAC was an efficient machine, working 1,440 times faster than a person on a calculator.

How **powerful** were the **first** computers?

Launched in **1946**, **ENIAC** (Electronic Numerical Integrator and Computer) was one of the **earliest** computers. It could perform up to **357 calculations** in **one second**.

ENIAC would take more than **20 years** to perform the same tasks as an **iPad** can in **1 second**.

An **iPad** can perform 22 billion operations in a single second.

00:01

Start   Pause

Computers have decreased in size, but increased in capability. Miniature computers are built into phones, cars, cameras, and all sorts of other devices. These are light, easy to operate, and able to perform a huge range of useful functions at incredibly fast speeds.

FAST FACTS

ENIAC was not the first computer: that was Colossus, used from 1943 by British code-breakers during World War II. Despite its name, Colossus was much smaller than ENIAC. While ENIAC measured 30 ft x 50 ft (9 m x 15 m), Colossus was less than one-ninth of the size.

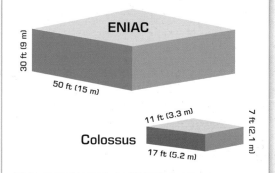

ENIAC

30 ft (9 m)

50 ft (15 m)

11 ft (3.3 m)

Colossus

17 ft (5.2 m)

7 ft (2.1 m)

ENIAC weighed 30 tons (27 metric tons), which was heavier than five elephants. Colossus was less than 1.1 tons (1 metric ton).

How much paper does it take to print the world wide web?

The **world wide web** is the network of all the world's websites. Calculations suggest **136 billion sheets** of **letter-size paper** would be needed to print it all out.

If the A4 printouts of the world wide web were piled up, the stack would be taller than Earth.

Stack of paper:
8,450 miles
(13,600 km)

Height of Earth:
7,900 miles
(12,713 km)

PAPER RECYCLING

Making recycled sheets from used paper uses 40 percent less energy than making new paper from trees. Going paperless is the most tree-efficient of all!

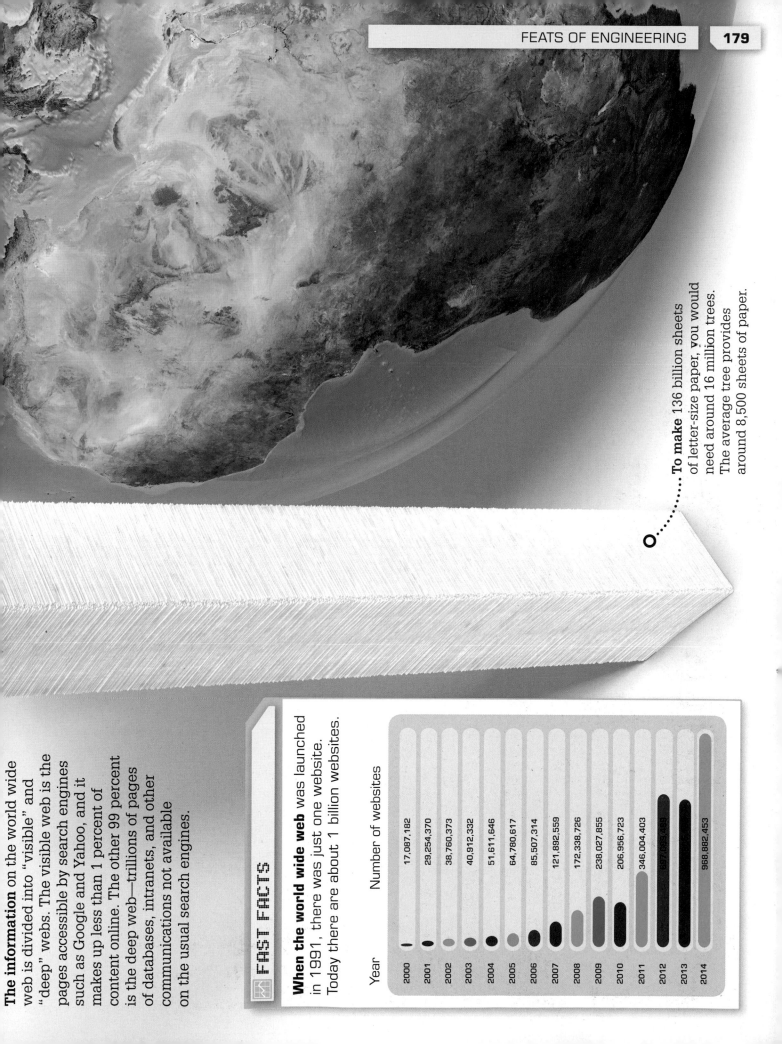

To make 136 billion sheets of letter-size paper, you would need around 16 million trees. The average tree provides around 8,500 sheets of paper.

The **information** on the world wide web is divided into "visible" and "deep" webs. The visible web is the pages accessible by search engines such as Google and Yahoo, and it makes up less than 1 percent of content online. The other 99 percent is the deep web—trillions of pages of databases, intranets, and other communications not available on the usual search engines.

FAST FACTS

When the world wide web was launched in 1991, there was just one website. Today there are about 1 billion websites.

Year	Number of websites
2000	17,087,182
2001	29,254,370
2002	38,760,373
2003	40,912,332
2004	51,611,646
2005	64,780,617
2006	85,507,314
2007	121,892,559
2008	172,338,726
2009	238,027,855
2010	206,956,723
2011	346,004,403
2012	697,089,489
2013	
2014	968,882,453

How **heavy** is the **internet?**

The **internet** runs on **electricity**, and the **electrons** involved are virtually **weightless**. Estimates suggest that the internet's **trillions** of active electrons weigh only **2 oz** (50–60 g).

SUBATOMIC PARTICLES

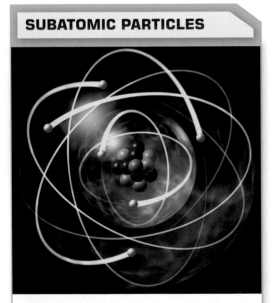

Atoms are made up of tiny particles called protons, neutrons, and electrons. Each atom has a nucleus (center) made up of protons and neutrons, while electrons spin around the nucleus.

This apricot is about 2 in (5 cm) across.

A USB ("Universal Serial Bus") is used to plug electronic devices into a computer or a power socket.

The **internet weighs about as much as an apricot.**

FAST FACTS

Some experts estimate the weight of all the data on the internet (including photographs, emails, and social media messages) totals the same weight as a grain of sand.

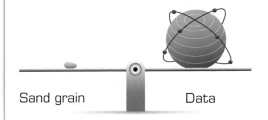

Sand grain   Data

Internet speed, or bandwidth, is measured in megabits per second (Mbps). Technically, 4 Mbps is not four times faster than 1 Mbps. Bandwidth is like a highway: 1 Mpbs means there is one lane of traffic, and 4 Mpbs means there are four lanes that the same amount of traffic can use. It all moves at the same speed, but more arrives at the same time.

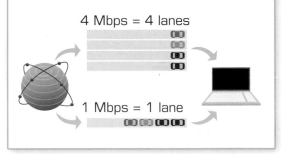

4 Mbps = 4 lanes

1 Mbps = 1 lane

An electron is a mind-blowingly miniscule particle of electricity with minimal mass. Though the content of the internet is vast, the electrons that run it have almost no mass, which is why the total internet weighs so little.

An apricot has the same mass as the electrons that carry the internet's 5 million terabytes of online information.

What's the largest diamond?

The Cullinan was bought for the equivalent of nearly 31 gold bars.

The **Cullinan** is the **largest uncut diamond** ever found. At just over **4 in** (10.5 cm) across at its widest, it is about the **size** of a **man's fist**.

📊 FAST FACTS

The Cullinan was cut into nine large diamonds and 96 smaller polished stones.

The uncut diamond weighed 3,106 carats. One carat is 0.007 oz (0.2 g), so the diamond weighed 21.9 oz (621.35 g)—about as much as a kitten.

Each gold bar has a value of $800,000 (£560,000), which is a high price. If the price dropped to $500,000 (£350,000), it would take nearly 50 bars to buy the diamond.

The uncut Cullinan was sold in 1905 for $727,500 (£150,000), which is worth more than $24.6 million (£16 million) in today's money.

TERMITE TREASURE

The richest diamond deposit, at Jwaneng in Botswana, was found thanks to termites. Burrowing into the ground, the insects brought soil to the surface that was tested and revealed minerals linked to diamonds and gold.

The Cullinan diamond was discovered in a diamond mine in Cullinan, South Africa, in the early 20th century. The largest diamond cut from the stone is the Great Star of Africa, which weighs 530 carats (3.7 oz/106 g) and is part of the UK's Crown Jewels.

What's the most **expensive** object ever **built?**

The most expensive man-made object is the **International Space Station**, which is in orbit **240 miles** (390 km) above Earth. Its final cost will be more than **$114 billion** (£80.7 billion).

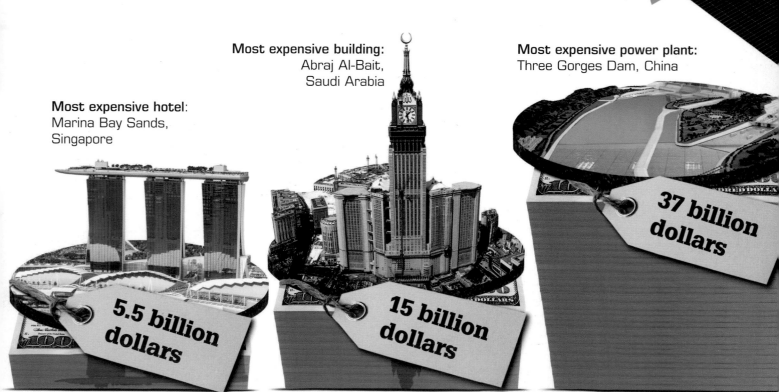

There are **12 large solar panels** powering the space station.

Most expensive hotel:
Marina Bay Sands, Singapore

Most expensive building:
Abraj Al-Bait, Saudi Arabia

Most expensive power plant:
Three Gorges Dam, China

5.5 billion dollars

15 billion dollars

37 billion dollars

Since its launch in 1998, the ISS has made more than 100,000 circuits of Earth and traveled in excess of 2.7 billion miles (4.3 billion km). Astronauts stay on board for months at a time.

114 billion dollars

The ISS orbits Earth every 90 minutes, traveling at 17,240 mph (27,750 kph).

The ISS is more than seven times costlier than the most expensive building on Earth.

FAST FACTS

The USA has sent 141 visitors to the ISS, more than any other country in the world.

Number of visitors to the ISS

USA: 141
Russia: 44
Europe: 17
Canada: 7
Japan: 7
Other: 5

From end to end, the ISS measures 357 ft (109 m), which is slightly larger than the length of an average soccer field.

FANTASY ISLANDS

Artificial islands are also very costly construction projects. Dubai's Palm Jumeirah cost about $12 billion to build, and there are more islands in progress.

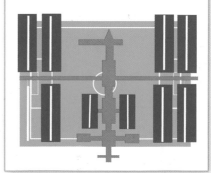

Money data

RICHEST RESIDENTS

This chart shows the richest nations measured by **GDP** (gross domestic product; the value of its goods and services) **per person** (if the GDP were shared equally among its population). According to this, the richest place to live is Qatar.

THOUSANDS OF DOLLARS

150

100

50

QATAR · MACAU · LUXEMBOURG · SINGAPORE · KUWAIT · BRUNEI · U A E · NORWAY · SWITZERLAND · HONG KONG

THE RICH GET RICHER

The richest **62** people in the world (only nine of whom are women) are as wealthy as half of the world's population. In 2010, the same proportion of wealth was in the hands of **388** people.

GLOBAL WEALTH PYRAMID

The global wealth pyramid demonstrates how many people have how much wealth. At the bottom of the pyramid, the majority of the world's population **(69.8 percent)** have the lowest amount of money **(less than $10,000)**.

At the very top of the pyramid, **35 million people** (a tiny **0.7 percent** of the world's population) own more than **$1 million**. In fact, the total amount owned by the **35 million** people is a whopping **$115.9 trillion.**

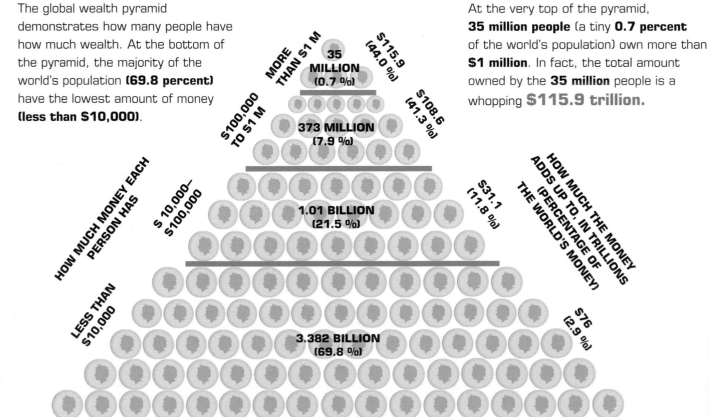

HOW MUCH MONEY EACH PERSON HAS

HOW MUCH THE MONEY ADDS UP TO, IN TRILLIONS (PERCENTAGE OF THE WORLD'S MONEY)

MORE THAN $1 M — 35 MILLION (0.7 %) — $115.9 (44.0 %)

$100,000 TO $1 M — 373 MILLION (7.9 %) — $108.6 (41.3 %)

$10,000– $100,000 — 1.01 BILLION (21.5 %) — $31.1 (11.8 %)

LESS THAN $10,000 — 3.382 BILLION (69.8 %) — $76 (2.9 %)

HOW MANY ADULTS HAVE THIS AMOUNT OF MONEY (PERCENTAGE OF WORLD POPULATION)

HOW **MUCH MONEY** IS THERE?

The total value of the world's money is **$81.21 trillion**. This includes **coins**, **banknotes**, and *money registered to bank accounts*. However, the value of all the world's *actual* coins and banknotes is just **$5 trillion**!

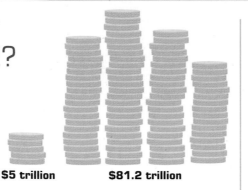

$5 trillion $81.2 trillion

PERSON ON THE MOST **MONEY**

Queen Elizabeth II of the UK holds the record for appearing on more currency than any other person. Her portrait is on the currency of at least **35** different countries.

PLAYING WITH MONEY

The amount of money in a Monopoly game is **$15,140**. That's **40** each of **$1, $5,** and **$10** bills; **50 $20** bills; **30 $50** bills; and **20** each of **$100** and **$500** bills. More than **250 million** games have been sold in **103** countries and **37** languages.

BIG MONEY

The **biggest** gold coin in the world was made by the **Perth Mint** in **Australia** in 2012. It is **31½ in** (80 cm) aross, **4¾ in** (12 cm) thick, and weighs **1.1 tons** (1 metric ton). Containing **99.99 percent** pure gold, it is the most valuable gold bullion coin in the world.

UNDER THE **HAMMER**

Most expensive painting: Picasso's *Women of Algiers*, sold in 2015 for **$179.4 million** (£102.6 million)

Most expensive sculpture: Giacometti's *Pointing Man*, sold in 2015 for **$141.3 million** (£90.5 million)

Most expensive instrument: *Lady Blunt* Stradivarius violin made in 1721, sold online in 2011 for **$15.9 million** (£9.8 million)

EVEN BIGGER MONEY!

Ceremonial money called **Rai** is used on the island of Yap (part of the Solomon Islands). The huge limestone discs are **12 ft** (3.6 m) across, **1½ ft** (0.5m) **thick,** and weigh **4.4 tons** (4 metric tons).

INDEX

ACKNOWLEDGMENTS

Dorling Kindersley would like to thank: Robert Dinwiddie, Derek Harvey, Chris Hawkes, Ben Morgan, and Richard Walker for fact checking; Jessica Cawthra, Bahja Norwood, and Rona Skene for editorial assistance.

The publisher would like to thank the following for their kind permission to reproduce their photographs:

(Key: a-above; b-below/bottom; c-center; f-far; l-left; r-right; t-top)

2 Alamy Images: dpa picture alliance archive (br/Chameleon). **Dreamstime.com:** Kmitu (br/Pencil); Stnazkul (tr). **3 Caters News Agency:** (tl). **Corbis:** Jörg Carstensen / dpa (tr). **Science Photo Library:** Gustoimages (tc). **4-5 Dreamstime.com:** Stnazkul. **8 Corbis:** Jeff Vanuga (clb). **11 Corbis:** Gary Bell (tr). **13 Alamy Images:** ColsTravel (tr). **14 Corbis:** Armin Weigel / Epa (clb). **16 Dreamstime.com:** Joseph Gough (clb); Xi Zhang (cr/Used Twice). **17 123RF.com:** Aaron Amat (tr). **18 Dreamstime.com:** Stnazkul (clb). **20 Corbis:** 68 / Ocean (bc). **Dreamstime.com:** Joggie Botma (br). **21 Alamy Images:** Joggie Botma (bl). **Dreamstime.com:** Joggie Botma (bc). **24 Corbis:** Bettmann (clb/Venus); Walter Myers / Stocktrek Images (c). **Dreamstime.com:** Yiannos1 (clb/Globe). **NASA:** Johns Hopkins University Applied Physics Laboratory / Arizona State University / Carnegie Institution of Washington (clb/Mercury). **U.S. Geological Survey:** USGS Astrogeology Science Center (clb/Valles Marineris). **25 Dreamstime.com:** Elisanth (ca, fcrb). **NASA:** JPL (cb); JPL / Space Science Institute (clb); Erich Karkoschka, University of Arizona (crb); Goddard / Lunar Reconnaissance Orbiter (tr). **27 Getty Images:** ESA (cr). **Pascal Henry,www.lesud.com:** (b/Planets). **28-29 Dreamstime.com:** Panaceadoll (c). **Pascal Henry,www.lesud.com:** (All planets). **30-31 Dreamstime.com:** Igor Terekhov (All kitchen scales used on the spread). **TurboSquid:** atolyee84 (cra/All oranges used on the spread). **30 Dreamstime.com:** Anna1311 (ca); Katerina Kovaleva (Orange quarter pieces on the spread). **NASA:** (clb); Johns Hopkins University Applied Physics Laboratory / Carnegie Institution of Washington (cl); JPL (c); NASA Goddard Space Flight Center Image by Reto Stöckli (land surface, shallow water, clouds). Enhancements by Robert Simmon (ocean color, compositing, 3D globes, animation). Data and technical support: MODIS Land Group; MODIS Science Data Support Team; MODIS Atmosphere Group; MODIS Ocean Group Additional data: USGS EROS Data Center (topography); USGS Terrestrial Remote Sensing Flagstaff Field Center (Antarctica); Defense Meteorological Satellite Program (city lights). (bc); JPL-Caltech (cr). **31 Dreamstime.com:** Steven Cukrov (All Clementines in Wood Crate used on the spread). **NASA:** (bl); SDO (tl). **Pascal Henry,www.lesud.com:** (c, br). **33 NASA:** Johns Hopkins University Applied Physics Laboratory / Southwest Research Institute (tr). **34-35 Dreamstime.com:** Yiannos1 (All Earth Globes). **35 NASA:** Science (bc). **36 ESA:** Rosetta / MPS for OSIRIS Team MPS / UPD / LAM / IAA / SSO / INTA / UPM / DASP / IDA (clb, bl). **36-37 Dreamstime.com:** Tomas Griger (b). **ESA:** Rosetta / MPS for OSIRIS Team MPS / UPD / LAM / IAA / SSO / INTA / UPM / DASP / IDA (Comet). **38-39 ESA. 38 ESA:** (bl). **42-43 Caters News Agency. 44-45 Alamy Images:** WENN Ltd. (b). **45 Corbis:** Pete Oxford / Minden Pictures (tr). **47 Getty Images:** Austin Hargrave / Barcroft Media (crb). **49 Corbis:** Hiroya Minakuchi / Minden Pictures (tr). **50-51 Dreamstime.com:** Jamie Cross (All the stopwatches used on the spread); Vladimir Surkov (Underwater background used on the spread). **50 Dreamstime.com:** Rostislav Ageev (br); Fotosforthought (bl); Michael Price (bc/Orca); Kotomiti_okuma (bc/Penguin). **Getty Images:** Andrey Nekrasov (cl). **51 Corbis:** DLILLC (clb). **Dreamstime.com:** Valentyna Chukhlyebova (cb); Stephanie Starr (tr). **Justin Hart:** (cr). **55 Corbis:** Ingo Arndt / Minden Pictures (bl). **Mary Evans Picture Library:** Natural History Museum (crb). **56 Dreamstime.com:** Daniel Cole; Lukas Gojda (Water Splash). **56-57 Dreamstime.com:** Annkozar (Water). **57 Dreamstime.com:** Isselee. **58 Dreamstime.com:** Pti4kafoto (clb). **58-59 Dreamstime.com:** Christian Delbert (t); Thomas Theodore (b). **60-61 Dorling Kindersley:** Thackeray Medical Museum (Bottles used on the spread). **60 Alamy Images:** Rieger Bertrand / Hemis (bl). **Photoshot:** Tobias Bernhard / NHPA (br). **61 Alamy Images:** Norman Price (bl). **Dreamstime.com:** Mkojot (c). **Getty Images:** Auscape (crb). **62 Corbis:** David Scharf (clb). **Dreamstime.com:** Stephen Sweet (All the drums used on the spread). **Science Photo Library:** Eye Of Science (cr). **62-63 Dreamstime.com:** Wektorygrafika (b). **63 Dreamstime.com:** Tofuxs (cb). **Sean McCann:** (cl). **64 Corbis:** Colin Stinson / Demotix (clb). **64-65 Blue whale heart model by Human Dynamo Workshop Ltd - humandynamo.co.nz:** (tc). **66 Alamy Images:** Ann and Steve Toon (tl). **66-67 Alamy Images:** NSP-RF. **67 Alamy Images:** Ann and Steve Toon (cb); WILDLIFE GmbH (cl). **Dreamstime.com:** Nigel Spooner (clb); Maximiliane Wagner (tr). **70-71 Alamy Images:** Paul Brown. **70 123RF.com:** marigranula (clb). **72 Corbis:** Thomas Marent / Minden Pictures (cla). **74-75 Alamy Images:** dpa picture alliance archive. **75 Dreamstime.com:** Cathy Keifer (tr); Kmitu (b). **76 Corbis:** Peter Ginter / Science Faction (clb). **78 Photoshot:** Mark Conlin / Oceans-Image (bc). **80-81 Alamy Images:** Don Mason / CORBIS / Flirt (Big Bees). **FLPA:** Ingo Arndt / Minden Pictures. **81 Alamy Images:** James Williamson (crb). **Corbis:** Maximilian Stock Ltd / photocuisine (bl). **82 Corbis:** Holger Hollemann / epa (clb). **84 Dreamstime.com:** Michel Bussieres (tl); Darkbird77 (br). **Getty Images:** Jena Ardell (tr). **85 Alamy Images:** Patrick Lynch (cb). **86 Science Photo Library:** Walter Myers (tl). **88-89 123RF.com:** Glenn Young. **88 naturepl.com:** Visuals Unlimited (bl). **91 Getty Images:** DigitalGlobe / ScapeWare3d (crb). **92 123RF.com:** Varga Andras (crb). **Corbis:** Wild Wonders of Europe / Lundgren / Nature Picture Library (c). **Getty Images:** Picture by Tambako the Jaguar (bl); Digital Zoo (bc). **92-92 Dreamstime.com:** Angelo Gilardelli (Mattresses). **92-93 Dreamstime.com:** Jamie Cross (Stopwatch); Angelo Gilardelli (Purple Mattresses). **93 Dreamstime.com:** Chase Clausen (cl); Artem Svystun (cra). **Getty Images:** Natphotos (bl). **94-95 Dreamstime.com:** Klausmeierklaus (b). **94 Corbis:** Laurent Giraudou (c). **98-99 Science Photo Library:** Gustoimages. **100 Dreamstime.com:** Mantinov (clb). **101 Corbis:** Jurgen Ziewe / Ikon Images (cr). **102 Dreamstime.com:** 1enchik (cb); Diego Barucco (clb); Mopic (bl). **104-105 Dreamstime.com:** Rawpixelimages (t/Used multiple times on the spread). **104 Dreamstime.com:** Monkey Business Images (crb/Used multiple times on the spread); Hongqi Zhang (aka Michael Zhang) (cra/Used multiple times on the spread); Get4net (cr/Used multiple times on the spread). **105 Dreamstime.com:** Elena Elisseeva (cl/Used multiple times on the spread); Alexander Raths (cla/Used multiple times on the spread, c/Used multiple times on the spread); Andres Rodriguez (clb/Used multiple times on the spread); Itsmejust (cr); Tmcphotos (cb/Used multiple times on the spread). **106 Getty Images:** Greg Wood / AFP (br). **110 Corbis:** Michael Macor / San Francisco Chronicle (clb). **113 Dreamstime.com:** Kevin Panizza (bl). **114-115 Dreamstime.com:** Dzmitri Mikhaltsov (c). **114 Alamy Images:** blickwinkel (bc). **115 Dreamstime.com:** Tracy King (cl). **118-119 Dreamstime.com:** Rakjung2 (cb). **119 123RF.com:** Aaron Amat (t). **Dreamstime.com:** Jacek Sopotnicki (br). **120 Corbis:** William Radcliffe / Science Faction (clb). **121 Dreamstime.com:** William Roberts (cla, tc). **125 Getty Images:** Thomas Kokta (tr). **126-127 Dreamstime.com:** Glenn Price (c). **127 Alamy Images:** Wayne Farrell (tr); The Oxfordshire Chilli Garden (r/Chilli). **Dreamstime.com:** Ron Sumners (r/Flame). **128-129 Alamy Images:** Arterra Picture Library (c). **128 Alamy Images:** Arterra Picture Library (cra). **Dreamstime.com:** Kevin Carden (clb). **129 Alamy Images:** Hemis (bl); Arterra Picture Library (cla, tl, tc, ca). **130 123RF.com:** Evgeny Karandaev (bl); nito500 (bc); Thanakrit Yomthaisong (br). **Dreamstime.com:** Baibaz (fbl). **130-131 123RF.com:** zdravinjo (b/All sugar cubes used on the spread). **131 123RF.com:** bagwold (bc); Evgeny Karandaev (bl). **Dreamstime.com:** Lasse Kristensen (br). **132 Alamy Images:** dbimages (clb). **Dreamstime.com:** Roman Samokhin (br). **132-133 123RF.com:** Natalia Merzlyakova. **135 Getty Images:** STR / AFP (crb). **138-139 Corbis:** Jörg Carstensen / dpa. **140 Alamy Images:** GL Archive (clb). **140-141 Alamy Images:** Stefan Hofecker. Christophe Dedieu: (b/Harmony Of The Seas). **141 Rex by Shutterstock:** Erik Pendzich (b). **143 Getty Images:** Obank / Connellan / Barcroft Media (br). **144 Getty Images:** Mike Hewitt / Allsport (clb). **146-147 Dreamstime.com:** Konstantinos Moraitis (All mini cars used on the spread.). **Getty Images:** Peter Endig. **147 Alamy Images:** SPUTNIK (tr). **148-149 Jani Bryson:** (Photo of children used multiple times in the spread). **SD Model Makers:** (c). **149 Alamy Images:** LondonPhotos - Homer Sykes (bc). **151 TopFoto.co.uk:** PA Photos (tr). **153 Alamy Images:** Michael Jenner / Robertharding (crb). **154 Getty Images:** Rolf Hicker (cl). **158 Getty Images:** Tuul / robertharding (br). **Imaginechina:** Niu shupei (c). **159 123RF.com:** Peter Wollinga (cr). **Corbis:** Roger Wood (br). **Dreamstime.com:** Hecke01 (c); Klausmeierklaus (fbl); Pixattitude (bc). **160-161 Alamy Images:** Jonny White (b). **161 Dreamstime.com:** Olaf Speier (cl). **Getty Images:** Burazin / Photographer's Choice RF (cra). **162-163 TurboSquid:** squir (Golden Gate Bridge). **163 Salavat Fidai:** (cr). **166 NASA:** (cl). **170-171 Dreamstime.com:** Rangizzz (All clapboards used on the spread); Tsiumpa (All film reels used on the spread). **170 123RF.com:** Plengsak Chuensriwiroj (fcr). **171 123RF.com:** looooaooool (cl); Grigory Lukyanov (fcl). **Dreamstime.com:** Leonello Calvetti (c). **174-175 TurboSquid:** 3d_molier. **175 Alamy Images:** BSIP SA (tr). **TurboSquid:** 3d_molier (br). **176 Corbis:** Bettmann (l). **Rex by Shutterstock:** Imaginechina (tl). **177 Corbis:** Paul Hakimata / Phakimata (bl). **178 Corbis:** Franz-Peter Tschauner / dpa (bc). **178-179 Dreamstime.com:** Iulius Costache (cr). **180 Dreamstime.com:** Sashkinw (bc). **180-181 Dreamstime.com:** Atoss1 (c). **182-183 TurboSquid:** dzejsi models (Gold Bricks). **183 Alamy Images:** WENN Ltd (tl). **Getty Images:** Alexander Joe / AFP (tr). **184 Dreamstime.com:** Jjspring (br); Keechuan (bl). **Getty Images:** Mohammed Al-Shaikh / AFP (bc). **184-185 Dreamstime.com:** Leerodney Avison (All Dollar Bill Stacks used on the spread); Hannu Viitanen (All tags used on the spread). **NASA:** (t). **185 Corbis:** (cb)

All other images © Dorling Kindersley

For further information see: www.dkimages.com